# THE BOOKSHOPS OF LONDON

# THE BOOKSHOPS OF LONDON

The Comprehensive Guide for Book Lovers
in and around the Capital

EDITED BY
MATT
JACKSON

MAINSTREAM
PUBLISHING
EDINBURGH AND LONDON

This edition first published in Great Britain in 1999 by
MAINSTREAM PUBLISHING COMPANY (EDINBURGH) LTD
7 Albany Street
Edinburgh EH1 3UG

ISBN 1 84018 237 7

A catalogue record for this book is available from the British Library

Typeset in Sabon
Printed and bound in Great Britain by Creative Print Design Ltd

# Contents

# Introduction

Welcome to the new edition of *The Bookshops of London*. Now completely revised and updated, it is the only guide to cover all bookshops – new, secondhand, antiquarian and specialist – in central, inner and outer London.

Its focus is the wealth of specialist booksellers in and around the capital but it also covers those who are best at being generalists, whether as part of a national chain or as local community bookshops. Only bookshops open to the public are included, although there are a couple of exceptions where it's advisable to call before visiting but they have been included in this guide because of their unique specialisation. To be included as a bookshop books must be the main product sold, or they must carry a specialist range of books alongside other associated products. Shops falling into the latter category are often overlooked when searching for a book of a specialist nature, so this guide will hopefully point you in the right direction.

The shops are presented by main subject specialisation and the listings are intended to be descriptive rather than judgemental. We all have our favourite bookshops and what is a goldmine to someone may be a heap of rubbish to someone else. We take the view that if a shop is particularly poor for some obvious reason or there are better alternatives available, then it's more useful to concentrate on bookshops people will enjoy visiting. The intention is simply to provide a feel for the character of a bookshop as well as providing essential facts.

Where a section heading covers a wide scope of subjects a selection of indvidual subjects covered is listed at the start. The bookshops are then featured alphabetically by name within the section. Categorising bookshops into one of 23 subject sections is not always a straightforward task and inevitably there is an occasional element of overlap where a shop could fall into two categories. Shops are cross-referenced where appropriate and as a general rule it is the main subject specialisation that determines where the shop will be listed – a shop selling secondhand art books will therefore be listed under Art & Design, and so on. There is a separate section on the general chains but where an individual branch has a true specialisation, an entry will be found in the appropriate subject section.

The indices allow users to quickly locate shops by name and to identify all bookshops in a specific geographical area.

Whether you are involved in the book trade, a reader, collector, book buyer or book-loving visitor to London, we hope you find this new edition even more useful than the first. Enjoy.

# Academic

**Archaeology • Campus Shops •Cartography • Course Texts
Education •Genealogy •History • Homeopathy • Humanism • Law
Medical •Philosophy • Psychology • Science •Surveying • Technology**

## Blackwell's

| | |
|---|---|
| **Branch** | 100 Charing Cross Road |
| | London |
| | WC2H 0JG |
| **Tel** | 020 7292 5100 |
| **Fax** | 020 7240 9665 |

**Web**
www.bookshop.blackwell.co.uk
**Email**
London@blackwellsbookshop.co.uk
**Opening hours**
Mon-Sat 9.30am – 8.30pm, Sun 12am – 6pm

Blackwell's attempt to establish a more general presence is a real contrast to nearby Books etc, Waterstone's and Foyles. The shop is much larger within than it appears from outside and has an altogether different feel than that of its neighbours. The academic focus is evident in every area of the shop although the range of general titles covers most of the basics.

| | |
|---|---|
| **Branch** | University Bookshop |
| | 158 Holloway Road |
| | London |
| | N7 8DD |
| **Tel** | 020 7700 4786 |
| **Fax** | 020 7700 7687 |

**Email**
unl@blackwellsbookshops.co.uk
**Opening hours**
Mon-Fri 9am – 5.30pm, Sat 10am – 5pm

Provides students at the University of North London with all their required texts and course books, as well as a smattering of more relaxing reading material.

**Branch**  University of North London
Ladbroke House
62-66 Highbury Grove
London
N5 2AD
**Tel**  020 7753 5087 ext. 5193
**Opening hours**
Mon-Fri 10am – 4pm (closed 2-3)

Located in the university building with a stock devoted exclusively to course texts.

**Branch**  University Bookshop
119-122 London Road
Elephant and Castle
London
SE1 6LF
**Tel**  020 7928 5378
**Fax**  020 7261 9536
**Opening hours**
Mon-Fri 9am – 6pm, Sat 10am – 5pm

Well-stocked college bookshop serving the needs of students at the South Bank University. Of particular note because of the extensive range of computer books.

**Branch**  South Bank University
Wandsworth Road
London
SW8 2JZ
**Tel**  020 7815 8302
**Fax**  020 7815 8302
**Email**
sbu@blackwellsbookshops.co.uk
**Opening hours**
Mon-Fri 9.30am – 5.30pm (closed 2-3)

Concentrates on the specialist areas of building construction, architecture, law and property.

**Branch**  Royal Free Hospital
School of Medicine
Rowland Hill Street
London
NW3 2PF
**Tel**  020 7830 2180
**Fax**  020 7830 2180
**Opening hours**
Mon-Fri 10am – 3pm

Medical and nursing texts within the Royal Free Hospital library.

**Branch**  King's College School of
Medicine & Dentistry
Bessemer Road
London
SE5 9PJ
**Tel**  020 7346 4074
**Fax**  020 7346 4074
**Opening hours**
Mon-Fri 10am – 5pm

The second of Blackwell's specialist medical outlets.

# BMJ Bookshop

**Address**  Burton Street
London
WC1H 9JR
**Tel**  020 7383 6244
**Fax**  020 7383 6455
**Web**
www.bmjbookshop.com
**Email**
orders@bmjbookshop.com
**Opening hours**
Mon-Fri 9.30am – 5pm

The bookshop of the British Medical Association, located inside the BMJ building, has a comprehensive range of stock encompassing all areas of medicine and related fields. For students, professionals and members elsewhere in the country a postage-free mail order service is in operation.

# Boffin Book Service

**Address**   24 Walton Street
Walton-on-the-Hill
Surrey
KT20 7RT
**Tel**   01737 812727/812676
**Fax**   01737 813526
**Email**
salesteam@boffinbooks.demon.co.uk
**Opening hours**
Mon-Sat 9am – 5.30pm (Weds closed)
**Services**
Mail order, catalogues

Originally founded as a mail order company, Boffin have recently opened a shop in the quiet main street of Walton. Specialising in medical and veterinary books, they also carry a small range of general titles.

# City Lit Bookshop

**Address**   City Literary Institute
16 Stukeley Street
London
WC2B 5LJ
**Tel**   020 7405 3110

*See Languages*

# College Bookshop

**Address**   Newham Community
College
East Ham Centre
High Street South
London
E6 4ER
**Tel**   020 8472 9946
**Opening hours**
Mon-Thurs 9am – 3.30pm, Fri 9am – 1pm

Caters for the needs of students at the college with a selection of course texts and other academic subjects.

# Construction Books

**Address**   29 Leslie Park Road
Croydon
Surrey
CR0 6TN
**Tel**   020 8239 1300

*See Art & Design*

# Dillons Bookstore

**Address**   82 Gower Street
London
WC1E 6EQ
**Tel**   020 7636 1577/7467 1698
**Fax**   020 7580 7680

*See General*

# Faculty Books

**Address**   Middlesex Business School
The Hendon Campus
The Burroughs
London
NW4 4BT
**Tel**   020 8202 3593
**Email**
facultybooks@compuserve.com
**Opening hours**
Mon-Fri 10am – 4pm (Thurs 10am – 6.30pm)

Specialises in business and law books.

# Guildhall Library Bookshop

**Address**   Aldermanbury
London
EC2P 2EJ
**Tel**   020 7332 1858

**Fax**    020 7600 3384
**Email**
bookshop@ms.corpoflondon.gov.uk
**Opening hours**
Mon-Fri 9.30am – 4.45pm

Guildhall Library was founded over 400 years ago and is the major reference source library for London history. The stock range covers all aspect of London life and contains a vast number of maps dating from the 1500s to the modern day.

## Hammicks Legal Bookshop

**Branch**  191-192 Fleet Street
          London
          EC4A 2AH
**Tel**    020 7405 5711
**Fax**    020 7831 9849

*See Business*

## Harrow School Bookshop

**Address**  7 High Street
          Harrow-on-the-Hill
          Middlesex
          HA1 3HU
**Tel**    020 8869 1212
**Fax**    020 8423 3112
**Opening hours**
Mon-Fri 9am – 5pm, Sat 9am – noon, Sun 1pm – 5pm

Textbooks, educational titles and gifts branded with the school crest.

## Havering College Bookshop

**Address**  Ardleigh Green Road
          Hornchurch
          Essex
**Tel**    01708 452563
**Opening hours**
Term-time only – phone first

Located within the college with most major academic subjects covered.

## Heal Services

**Address**  26 Clarendon Rise
          London
          SE13 4EY
**Tel**    020 8297 1661

*See Mind, Body & Spirit*

## Intermediate Technology

**Address**  103-105 Southampton Row
          London
          WC1B 4HH
**Tel**    020 7436 9761
**Fax**    020 7436 2013

*See Environment & Nature*

## Jubilee Books

**Address**  23 Greenwich High Road
          London
          SE10
**Tel**    020 8692 2332
**Fax**    020 8692 0734
**Web**
www.jubilee-books.co.uk
**Email**
enquiries@jubilee-books.co.uk
**Opening hours**
Mon-Fri 10am – 6pm

Jubilee deals with the specialist educational requirements of teachers, libraries and schools. The main stock is concentrated on all the national curriculum texts. Friendly staff make visitors welcome and the service is expert.

## H Karnac

**Branch**  58 Gloucester Road
London
SW7 4QY
**Tel**  020 7584 3303
**Fax**  020 7823 7743
**Web**
www.karnacbooks.com
**Email**
books@karnac.demon.co.uk
**Opening hours**
Mon-Sat 9am – 6pm

**Branch**  118 Finchley Road
London
NW3 5HJ
**Tel**  020 7431 1075
**Opening hours**
Mon-Sat 9am – 6pm
**Services**
Mail order, catalogues

This specialist bookseller and publisher of international repute carries a comprehensive array of books on psychoanalysis, analytical psychology, child care and the family, psychotherapy, philosophy and gender studies. Allied topics are equally well covered with special sections on books related to childhood problems, sexual abuse and eating disorders. Karnac's publishing activities encompass original texts and translations in their specialist fields, having previously earned a reputation for keeping available classics of psychoanalytical writing. The mail order business is handled from Gloucester Road.

## King's Fund Bookshop

**Address**  11-13 Cavendish Square
London
W1M 0AN
**Tel**  020 7307 2591
**Fax**  020 7307 2805
**Web**
www.kingsfund.org.uk
**Email**
cmorris@kingsfund.org.uk
**Opening hours**
Mon-Fri 9.30am – 5.30pm
**Services**
Mail order, catalogues

Founded by King Edward VII to promote the health and social care of London's residents, the King's Fund organisation occupies two magnificent 18th-century buildings in Cavendish Square and boasts an Epstein sculpture of the crucifixion at the entrance. Topics covered include health and social issues, disability, mental health, care in the community and nursing.

## Lamb's Bookshop

**Address**  21 Store Street
London
WC1E 7DH
**Tel**  020 7580 7632/7633
**Fax**  020 7580 8970
**Email**
lambs@globalnet.co.uk
**Opening hours**
Mon-Fri 9am – 6pm, Sat noon – 4pm

Primarily a legal and medical books specialist with expert staff on hand to deal with any query. Lamb's also cover legal fields with an emphasis on intellectual property, media and internet law. On the medical side they are particularly expert in the areas of public health, tropical medicine and epidemiology.

## Law Books Online

**Address** 29 Leslie Park Road
Croydon
Surrey
CR0 6TN
**Tel** 020 8239 1400
**Opening hours**
Mon-Fri 9am – 6pm, Sat 10am – 2pm
**Services**
Mail order

Housed in the same building as Construction Books, they are equally expert though they deal exclusively in books on law.

## Law Society Shop

**Address** 113 Chancery Lane
London
WC2A
**Tel** 020 7320 5640

*See Business*

## Marylebone Books

**Branch** University of Westminster
35 Marylebone Road
London
NW1 5LS
**Tel** 020 7911 5049
**Fax** 020 7911 5046
**Email**
bookshop@westminster.ac.uk
**Opening hours**
Mon-Thurs 9.30am – 6.30pm, Fri-Sat 9.30am – 5.30pm
**Services**
Mail order, catalogues

**Branch** University of Westminster
Harrow Campus
Watford Road
Northwick Park
Harrow
HA1 3TP
**Tel** 020 7911 5961
**Fax** 020 7911 5961
**Email**
bshophrw@westminster.ac.uk
**Opening hours**
Mon-Fri 10am – 6.30pm
**Services**
Mail order

A better-than-most campus bookshop with a well-chosen stock range covering management, business, economics, accounting, finance and computing with a genuine specialism in tourism and housing. The Harrow Campus outlet is equally well run with a bias towards media and cultural studies.

## Mencap Bookshop

**Address** 123 Golden Lane
London
EC1Y 0RT
**Tel** 020 7696 5569
**Fax** 020 7608 3254
**Web**
www.mencap.org.uk
**Email**
mencap.plu@dial.pipex.com
**Opening hours**
Mon-Fri 9am – 5.30pm
**Services**
Catalogues, mail order

Originally set up 25 years ago as an extension to the activities of the reference library. They have an extensive stock on the requirements of children and adults with special needs. The main subject categories covered are: carers, disabilities, education, health, integration, legal, recreation and therapy. The bookshop's catalogue lists and describes all publications under the main subject areas and also includes all of Mencap's own publications.

## Modern Book Co.

**Address**  19-21 Praed Street
Paddington
London
W2 1NP
**Tel**  020 7402 9176
**Fax**  020 7724 5736
**Web**
www.mbc.oaktree.co.uk
**Email**
books@mbc.oaktree.co.uk
**Opening hours**
Mon-Fri 9am – 5.30pm, Sat 9am – 1pm

Established over 60 years ago and family owned. The Modern Book Company has made a name for itself as a leading specialist in medical and technical books. Every department has its own expert on hand to meet the needs of students and professionals alike. The institutional and library supply department serves public bodies and industry worldwide. Apart from the medical and technical books they also carry a reasonable range of general books in all the popular subject areas.

## Museum Bookshop

**Address**  36 Great Russell Street
London

WC1B 3PP
**Tel**  020 7580 4086
**Fax**  020 7436 4364
**Email**
mbooks@btconnect.com
**Opening hours**
Mon-Sat 10am – 5.30pm
**Services**
Mail order

One of many bookshops in the enclave opposite the main entrance to the British Museum. After starting life as a generalist in 1978, Museum Books later developed into a specialist appropriate to its proximity to the British Museum. Packed with new and secondhand books in the specialist fields of Egyptology, archaeology, prehistoric and Roman Britain, classical history, museum studies and conservation, it has a slightly intimidating air but this shouldn't put anybody off browsing the extensive stocks.

## Oyez Straker

**Branch**  144-146 Fetter Lane
London
EC4 1BT
**Tel**  0870 7377370

**Branch**  15 Artillery Row
London
SW1P 1RT
**Tel**  0870 7377370

*See Business*

## RCOG Bookshop

**Address**  27 Sussex Place
Regent's Park
London
NW1 4RG

**Tel** 020 7772 6275
**Fax** 020 7724 5991
**Web**
www.rcog.org.uk
**Email**
bookshop@rcog.org.uk
**Opening hours**
Mon-Fri 9am – 5pm
**Services**
Mail order, catalogues

Originally founded as a service to fellows and trainees of the Royal College of Obstericians and Gynaecologists, it is now open to the public.

## Rudolf Steiner Bookshop

**Address** 35 Park Road
London
NW1 6XT
**Tel** 020 7724 7699
**Fax** 020 7724 4364
**Email**
rsh@cix.compulink.co.uk
**Opening hours**
Tues-Fri 10.30am – 6pm, Sat 10.30am – 5pm
**Services**
Mail order, catalogues

Located in a striking building just a short stroll from Baker Street underground, it is a cultural centre devoted to the work of Rudolph Steiner. Apart from a wide range of books they have a theatre, lending library and meeting rooms.

## Skoob Books

**Address** 15 Sicilian Avenue
Southampton Row
London

WC1A 2QH
**Tel** 020 7404 3063
**Fax** 020 7404 4398

*See Secondhand*

## Society of Genealogists

**Address** 14 Charterhouse Buildings
Goswell Road
London
EC1M 7BA
**Tel** 020 7253 5235
**Fax** 020 7250 1800
**Web**
www.sog.org.uk
**Email**
sales@sog.org.uk
**Opening hours**
Mon 10am – 5pm, Tues, Fri, Sat 10am – 6pm, Wed, Thurs 10am – 8pm
**Services**
Mail order, catalogues

A registered charity founded in 1911, the society started the bookshop when they moved to the Goswell Road location in the early 1980s. The stock consists of over 2,000 books on genealogy, family, local and general history. For those researching family trees from afar, the society claims to have the largest online family history bookshop in the world.

## Waterstone's

**Branch** Brunel University
Cleveland Road
Uxbridge
Middlesex
UB8 3PH
**Tel** 01895 257991

**Fax** 01895 232806

Once part of the Economists group, then a Dillons campus shop and now a Waterstone's. Still specialises in texts for students at Brunel.

**Branch** City University
Northampton Square
London
EC1V 0HB
**Tel** 020 7608 0706
**Fax** 020 7251 2813

Conveniently located close to the main entrance and covering all course material from computing to speech therapy.

**Branch** Goldsmiths' College
New Cross
London
SE14 6NW
**Tel** 020 8469 0262
**Fax** 020 8694 2279
**Opening hours**
Mon-Fri 9am – 7pm

University texts and reading in the arts, humanities and social sciences are the main focus with literature also featuring strongly.

**Branch** Imperial College
Imperial College Road
London
SW7 2A2
**Tel** 020 7589 3563
**Fax** 020 7591 3810

Science and technology, computing, maths, physics, geology and mining.

**Branch** London Guildhall
University
Calcutta House
Old Castle Street
London

E1 7NT
**Tel** 020 7247 0727
**Fax** 020 7247 0513

Course texts and some general items.

**Branch** Queen Mary and
Westfield College
329 Mile End Road
London
E1 4NT
**Tel** 020 8980 2554
**Fax** 020 8981 6774
**Opening hours**
Mon-Fri 9am – 5.30pm

Was a Dillons but now classed as a Waterstone's. Stocked with textbooks and student stationery.

**Branch** Royal Holloway College
University of London
Egham Hill
Egham
Surrey
TW20 0EX
**Tel** 01784 471272
**Fax** 01784 431369

Worth visiting purely to see the magnificent main college building. The range of academic texts and associated reading clearly saves students and lecturers alike from travelling into London for all their book needs.

**Branch** Thames Valley University
St Mary's Road
Waling
London
W5 5RF
**Tel** 020 8840 6205
**Fax** 020 8840 6729
**Opening hours**
Mon-Fri 9am – 5pm

Again, once a Dillons campus shop but now classed as a Waterstone's, with all the expected course texts.

**Branch**  University Bookshop
2 Brook Street
Kingston
Surrey
KT1 2HA
**Tel**  020 8546 7592
**Fax**  020 8974 9077

Campus shop at the sprawling Kingston University covering a wide range of topics studied on site such as design, fashion and business.

## Wellspring Bookshop

**Address**  Rudolf Steiner Books
5 New Oxford Street
London
W1CA 1BA
**Tel**  020 7405 6101
**Fax**  020 7405 0252
**Web**
www.mistral.co.uk/wellspringbooks

**Email**
nwillby@mistral.co.uk
**Opening hours**
Mon-Fri 10am – 5.30pm, Sat 11am – 5pm
**Services**
Mail order

A short walk from the British Museum. Wellspring was founded to promote the work of Rudolph Steiner and his world view – antroposophy (or the wisdom of man). Here you will find books on esoteric Christianity, education, biodynamic agriculture, cosmology, spiritual science and inner development.

## Wildy & Son

**Address**  16 Fleet Street
London
EC4Y 1AX
**Tel**  020 7353 3907
**Opening hours**
Mon-Fri 9am – 6pm, Sat 10am – 4pm

# Antiquarian

**Atlases • Art • Children's • Fine Bindings • First Editions • Horology
Leather Bindings • Maps • Medieval • Natural History • Travel**

## Arthur Probsthain

**Address**   41 Great Russell Street
              London
              WC1 3PL
**Tel**       020 7636 1096
**Fax**       020 7636 1096

*See Countries*

## Ash Rare Books

**Address**   25 Royal Exchange
              Threadneedle Street
              London
              EC3V 3LP
**Tel**       020 7626 2665
**Fax**       020 7623 9052
**Email**
worms@ashrare.demon.co.uk
**Opening hours**
Mon-Fri 10am – 5pm

**Services**
Mail order, catalogues

Two hundred years ago the Royal Exchange was one of the great centres of the book trade. It is now home to this approachable City-based antiquarian bookseller. The stock is small but highly selective and their customers include museums, libraries and collectors all over the world. Literature to 1900, fine binding and first editions are the main specialisations with a select range of antique maps and prints.

## Avril Noble

**Address**   2 Southampton Street
              London
              WC2E 7HA

**Tel** 020 7240 1970
**Opening hours**
Mon-Fri 10am – 5.30pm

Antiquarian books among the antique maps and prints in a location just off the Strand.

## Barrie Marks Ltd

**Address** 11 Laurier Road
Dartmouth Park
London
NW5 1SD
**Tel** 020 7482 5684
**Fax** 020 7284 3149
**Opening hours**
By appointment only

Appointments are required to view the stock of this specialised literary antiquarian bookseller. The stock is mainly centred around illustrated books, particularly children's.

## Beaumont Travel Books

**Address** 31 Museum Street
London
W1CA
**Tel** 020 7637 5862
**Fax** 020 7637 5862

*See Travel*

## Biblion

**Address** 1-7 Davies Mews
London
W1Y 2LP
**Tel** 020 7629 1374
**Fax** 020 7493 9344
**Web**
www.biblion.co.uk
**Email**
info@biblion.co.uk
**Opening hours**

Mon-Fri 10am – 6pm, Sat 11am – 4pm
**Services**
Mail order, catalogues

Opened in April 1999 and just a short walk from Bond Street underground station. Located in Gray antiques market, Biblion form the largest part of the antiquarian book market that has been established at this site. They stock a wide range of books, manuscripts and prints with prices from under £20 to over £20,000.

## Bibliopola

**Address** The Antique Market
13-25 Church Street
Marylebone
NW8
**Tel** 020 7724 7231
**Opening hours**
Tues-Sat 10am – 4pm

Established nearly 25 years ago, with experience that stretches back a further five years, means you will be pressed to find anywhere more knowledgeable on the subject of illustrated children's books and modern first editions.

## T A Cherrington

**Address** 81 Grosvenor Street
London
W1X 9DE
**Tel** 020 7493 1343
**Fax** 020 7499 2983
**Opening hours**
Mon-Fri 10am – 5.30pm

Antiquarian bookseller specialising in natural history, travel, architecture, colour plates, illustrated books, topography and costume.

## Classic Bindings

**Address**   61 Cambridge Street
Pimlico
London
SW1V 4PS
**Tel**   020 7834 5554
**Fax**   020 7630 6632
**Web**
www.classicbindings.net
**Email**
info@classicbindings.net
**Opening hours**
Mon-Fri 9.30am – 5.30pm
**Services**
Mail order, catalogues

Suppliers of fine and collectable 18th- and 19th-century complete sets and individual volumes. They are also library fittings specialists providing furniture, shelving and equipment along with a design service. For those who need shelves of books in a hurry, books can also be bought by the linear foot.

## Collinge and Clark

**Address**   18 Leigh Street
London
WC1H 9EW
**Tel**   020 7387 7105
**Fax**   020 7833 0335
**Opening hours**
Mon-Fri 11am – 6.30pm, Sat 11am – 3.30pm
**Services**
Catalogues

Humanities and the arts dominate with particularly fine illustrated books, history (books, pamphlets and ephemera) and private press

items to the fore. Prices match the excellent quality but there are plently of affordable leather-bound books to choose from.

## Christopher Edwards

**Address**   63 Jermyn Street
London
SW1Y 6LX
**Tel**   020 7495 4263
**Fax**   020 7495 4264
**Email**
chr.edwards@which.net
**Opening hours**
By appointment only
**Services**
Mail order, catalogues

Strictly antiquarian and rare books with a very small range of English literature and history to 1900. There are also some titles on continental history.

## Eastern Books

**Address**   81 Replingham Road
Southfields
London
SW18 5LU
**Tel**   020 8871 0880
**Fax**   020 8871 0880

*See Countries*

## Francis Edwards

**Address**   13 Great Newport Street
Charing Cross Road
London
WC2H 7JA
**Tel**   020 7379 7669
**Fax**   020 7836 5977

*See Transport & Military*

## Eurobooks Ltd

**Address**   4 Woodstock Street
London
W1
**Tel**   020 7403 2002
**Opening hours**
Mon-Fri 10am – 6pm, Sat 10am – 4pm

A pleasant book emporium just off
bustling Oxford Street and close to
Bond Street underground station.
All manner of antiquarian and
secondhand books are to be found
and it's a good shop for regular
browsing.

## Faircross Books

**Address**   Strand Antiques
166 Thames Street
Strand on the Green
London
W4 3QS
**Tel**   020 8994 1912
**Opening hours**
Mon-Sat 10.30am – 5.30pm

A good-sized area is devoted to
books in this popular antiques
market. Faircross are on the top
floor and offer a good collection of
general antiquarian and secondhand books across all the popular
subject areas. In keeping with the
antique furnishing theme leather-
bound volumes are sold by the
metre.

## Simon Finch Rare Books

**Address**   59 Maddox Street
London
W1R
**Tel**   020 7499 0974

**Opening hours**
Mon-Fri 10am – 6pm, Sat 10am – 5pm

A very attractive and nicely
designed shop close to Grosvenor
Square. The stock range majors in
illustrated books, colour plates, the
arts and travel with quality leather-
bound books lining the shelves.

## Fine Books Oriental Ltd

**Address**   38 Museum Street
London
WC1A 1LP
**Tel**   020 7242 5288
**Fax**   020 7242 5344

*See Countries*

## Finney, Micheal Books

**Address**   37 Museum Street
London
N1 8EA
**Tel**   020 7430 0202
**Opening hours**
Mon-Fri 10am –6pm, Sat 10am – 5pm

Mainly prints here but they do have
a small stock of antiquarian plate
books in the areas of natural
history, travel and architecture.

## Fisher and Sperr

**Address**   High Street
Highgate
London
N6 5JB
**Tel**   020 8340 7244
**Fax**   020 8348 4293
**Opening hours**
Mon-Sat 10am – 5pm

Housed in a majestic building in

Highgate Village, there is always something of interest in the window display to catch a browser's eye. Hardbacks dominate in all the popular subject areas but because of the volume of stock – and the turnover of incoming books – there is that booky feeling that somewhere in this warren of old books lies the volume you've been trying to lay your hands on for years. Mr Sperr is knowledgeable and helpful but his hearing is not as sharp as it once was, so you might have to disturb the tranquil atmosphere to make your wants known.

## Sam Fogg Rare Books

**Address**    35 St George Street
London
W1R 9FA
**Tel**    020 7495 2333
**Fax**    020 7495 2333
**Opening hours**
Mon-Fri 10am – 6pm

Appropriately located close to Sotheby's, this rarest of rare bookshops deals exclusively in medieval and illuminated manuscripts.

## Paul Foster Books

**Address**    119 Sheen Lane
East Sheen
London
SW14 8AE
**Tel**    020 8876 7424
**Fax**    020 8876 7424
**Email**
paulfosterbooks@btinternet.com
**Opening hours**
Mon-Sat 10.30am – 6pm
**Services**

Mail order, catalogues

Only 200 yards from Mortlake station and in business for almost ten years. The stock is general antiquarian with a bias towards first editions, children's illustrated books, art and fine bindings.

## Robert Frew

**Address**    106 Great Russell Street
London
WC1B 3NA
**Tel**    020 7580 2311
**Fax**    020 7580 2313
**Web**
www.robertfrewltd.demon.co.uk
**Email**
robertfrew@robertfrewltd.demon.co.uk
**Opening hours**
Mon-Fri 10am – 6pm, Sat 10am – 2pm
**Services**
Mail order, catalogues

Adjacent to the British Museum and dealing in quality antiquarian books at the more expensive end of the market, especially travel and particularly books on Greece and Levant. Glass cases protect the many sets of books.

## Adrian Harrington

**Address**    64a Kensington
Church Street
London
W8 4DB
**Tel**    020 7937 1465
**Fax**    020 7368 0912
**Web**
www.harringtonbooks
**Email**
rare@harringtonbooks.co.uk
**Opening hours**

Mon-Sat 10am – 6pm
**Services**
Mail order, catalogues

A large selection of leather-bound books, first editions and antique maps and prints decorate this splendid shop in this small but perfectly formed bookshop in Kensington Church Street. Among the many affordable modern firsts there are always a number of Ian Fleming Bond books for the collector. They also specialise in books by and about Winston Churchill.

## Peter Harrington

**Address**   100 Fulham Road
           Chelsea
           London
           SW3 6HS
**Tel**       020 7591 0220
**Fax**       020 7225 7054
**Web**
www.peter-harrington-books.com
**Email**
mail@peter-harrington-books.com
**Opening hours**
Mon-Sat 10am – 6pm
**Services**
Mail order, catalogues

Beautiful books in a beautiful shop with a firm emphasis on the higher end of the market for leather bindings, antiquarian and rare books.

## Harrison's Books

**Address**   Grays Mews
           Antiques Market
           1-7 Davies Mews
           London
           W1Y 1AR
**Tel**       020 7629 1374

**Opening hours**
Mon-Sat 10am – 6pm

Part of the books section of the Grays antique market. Along with Biblion they carry a wide-ranging stock of antiquarian, rare and general secondhand books from both the UK and around the world.

## P J Hilton

**Address**   12-14 Cecil Court
           Charing Cross Road
           London
           WC2N 4HE
**Tel**       020 7379 9825
**Opening hours**
Mon-Sat 10.30am – 6.30pm

An appealing range of secondhand and antiquarian books, especially English literature, both first editions and reading copies. The section devoted to recent acquisitions is worthy of regular inspection as is the section on theology and Christianity.

## Hosains Books

**Address**   25 Connaught Street
           London
           W2 2AY
**Tel**       020 7262 7900
**Fax**       020 7794 7127

*See Countries*

## Jarndyce Bookseller

**Address**   46 Great Russell Street
           London
           WC1B 3PA
**Tel**       020 7631 4220
**Fax**       020 7436 6544

**Opening hours**
Mon-Fri 9.30am – 5pm

Look for the brass plate on the wall of the house occupied by Randolph Caldecott, artist and book illustrator, from 1846 to 1886. Ring the bell to obtain access to the first-floor showroom but visit preferably by appointment to inspect the special pre-1900 range of fine, rare and interesting books. Victorian triple deckers, yellowbacks and Dickens first editions can be found here alongside English literature, social, economic and political history.

## Judith Lassalle

**Address**    7 Pierrepont Arcade
              Camden Passage
              London
              N1 8EF
**Tel**        020 7607 7121
**Fax**        020 7354 9344
**Opening hours**
Wed 7.30am – 4pm, Sat 9.30am – 4pm

Part of the busy Camden Passage antiques market off Islington's High Street. Contains an interesting collection of prints, children's games, optical toys, rocking horses and an eclectic selection of books on similar topics.

## London Antiquarian Book Arcade

**Address**    37 Great Russell Street
              London
              WC1B 3PP
**Tel**        020 7436 2054
**Fax**        020 7436 2057
**Email**

antiqarc@panix.com
**Opening hours**
Mon-Sat 10am – 6pm, Sun noon – 5pm

Operated by 'The Bohemian Bookworm' who runs a similar emporium in New York, this shop is billed as the 'gateway to the American bookmarket'. It's good for browsing through a regular set of subject areas and there is the added advantage of a free international booksearch if you can't find what you're looking for within.

## Maggs Brothers

**Address**    50 Berkeley Square
              London
              W1X 6EL
**Tel**        020 7493 7160
**Fax**        020 7499 2007
**Web**

www.maggs.com
**Opening hours**
Mon-Fri 9.30am – 5pm

A rare treat indeed and not to be missed on any tour of London's finest bookshops. Maggs Brothers was founded in 1853 and the family tradition continues with three Mr Maggses involved in the day-to-day running of this premier book business. Maggs moved to the present location, a magnificent Georgian residence – reputed to be one of the most haunted houses in London – on Berkeley Square in 1939. Each specialist department is staffed by experts who are on hand to deal with the needs of their discerning customers. The rarest first editions, manuscripts, fine bindings and an unparalleled collection of autographed material fill the floors in the most gracious manner. Unlike some other antiquarian specialists it is not all ivory towers and although the atmosphere is earnest and learned, it is far from elitist and all visitors are treated with equal courtesy, regardless of their spending power.

# Marlborough Rare Books

**Address** 144-146 New Bond Street
London
W1Y 9FD
**Tel** 020 7493 6993
**Fax** 020 7499 2479
**Web**
www.bibliocity.com/search/marlborough
**Email**
sales@mrb-books.co.uk
**Opening hours**
Mon-Fri 9.30am – 5.30pm
**Services**
Catalogues

Directly opposite Sotheby's and four floors up on fashionable New Bond Street. The arts, fine bindings, colour plates and topography are the main specialisations and although appointments are recommended to view the quality stock, it can also be perused electronically at any time by visiting Marlborough's web site.

# Pickering and Chatto

**Address** 36 St George Street
London
W1R 9FA
**Tel** 020 7930 2515

**Fax** 020 7930 8627
**Web**
www.pickering-chatto.com
**Email**
rarebooks@pickering-chatto.com
**Opening hours**
Mon-Fri 9.30am – 5.30pm
**Services**
Mail order, catalogues

Founded in 1820 by William Pickering, a leading publisher of the early 19th century, Pickering and Chatto is one of the oldest antiquarian booksellers in the capital. They specialise in economics, philosophy, medicine (including rare medical books dating from the 16th and 17th centuries) and science as well as the core business of English litera- ture. Frequent catalogues are produced but rarely contain anything under three figures.

# Jonathan Potter

**Address** 125 New Bond Street
London
W1Y 9AF
**Tel** 020 7491 3520
**Fax** 020 7491 9754
**Web**
www.jpmaps.co.uk
**Email**
jpmaps@ibm.net
**Opening hours**
Mon-Fri 10am – 6pm
**Services**
Mail order, catalogues

Located on the first floor, they have a magnificent range of antique maps, atlases and reference books on cartography. Exhibitions are often held here and a framing service is also available.

# Bernard Quatrich

**Address**   5-8 Lower John Street
Golden Square
London
W1R 4AU
**Tel**   020 7734 2983
**Fax**   020 7437 0967
**Web**
www.quatrich.com
**Email**
rarebooks@quatrich.com
**Opening hours**
Mon-Fri 9.30am – 5.30pm

Not really for the casual visitor who fancies a nice old leather-bound book. The stock is divided into separate sections and covers all classic antiquarian topics. A scholarly and earnest bookshop of international repute, they carry many rare manuscripts.

# John Randall Books

**Address**   47 Moreton Street
London
SW1V 2NY
**Tel**   020 7630 5331

*See Countries*

# Reg & Philip Remington

**Address**   18 Cecil Court
Charing Cross Road
London
WC2N 4HE
**Tel**   020 7836 9771
**Fax**   020 7497 2526

*See Travel*

# Bernard J Shapero Rare Books

**Address**   32 St George Street
London
W1R 0EA
**Tel**   020 7493 0876
**Fax**   020 7229 7860

*See Travel*

# Sims Reed Ltd

**Address**   43a Duke Street
London
SW1Y 6DD
**Tel**   020 7493 5660
**Fax**   020 7493 8468
**Services**
Mail order, catalogues

This shop stocks rare, out-of-print and new reference books on fine and applied art. It is not all historical as contemporary design is handsomely covered. Definitely not a place for the uninitiated.

# Henry Southeran

**Address**   2-5 Sackville Street
London
W1X 2DP
**Tel**   020 7439 6151
**Fax**   020 7434 2019
**Opening hours**
Mon-Fri 9.30am – 6pm, Sat 10am – 4pm
**Services**
Mail order, catalogues

The longest-established antiquarian bookseller in the country; founded in York in 1761 before moving to London in 1815. A large and elegant bookshop, although because of the inaccessibility of much of the stock, it is not as pleasing for browsing as it would appear from outside. Rare and antique prints accompany the rare and antique books.

## Storey's

**Address**  3 Cecil Court
Charing Cross Road
London
WC2N 4EZ
**Tel**  020 7836 3777
**Fax**  020 7836 3788
**Email**
storeysltd@btinternet.com
**Opening hours**
Mon-Sat 10am – 6pm
**Services**
Catalogues

Specialising in prints, maps and engravings in military and naval subjects with a small selection of rare books and fine bindings.

## Roger Turner Books

**Address**  22 Nelson Road
Greenwich
London
SE10 9JB
**Tel**  020 8853 5271

**Fax**  020 8853 5271
**Opening hours**
Thurs, Fri 10am – 6pm
**Services**
Mail order, catalogues

A very specialised stock awaits the visitor and collector. Horology, especially books on sundials, history of science and scientific instruments, linguistics and Germanic studies, are all to be found here.

## Tooley Adams and Co.

**Address**  13 Cecil Court
Charing Cross Road
London
WC2N 4EZ
**Tel**  020 7240 4406
**Fax**  020 7240 8058
**Opening hours**
Mon-Fri 9am – 5pm

R.V. Tooley, one of the original founders, was author of many authoritative works on the subject of antique maps and atlases, so it is not surprising to learn that the current business claims to hold one of the largest stocks of antiquarian maps and atlases in the world.

# Art & Design

**Applied Arts • Architecture • Bookbinding • Building • Calligraphy Design • Fine Art • Graphics • Interiors • Photography • Sculpture**

## Alison Knox Bookseller

**Address**   53 Exmouth Market
            London
            EC1R 4QL
**Tel**       020 7833 0591

*See Secondhand*

## Atrium Bookshop

**Address**   5 Cork Street
            London
            W1X 1PB
**Tel**       020 7495 0073
**Fax**       020 7409 7417
**Opening hours**
Mon-Fri 10am – 6pm, Sat 10am – 4pm
**Services**
Mail order, catalogues

Owned by Christie's, Atrium specialise in all aspects of fine and decorative arts and architecture. It is a light and friendly shop with knowledgeable staff, set in the middle of some of London's best contemporary art galleries and just a couple of minutes from the Royal Academy of Arts.

## Book Art and Architecture

**Address**   12 Woburn Walk
            London
            WC1H 0JL
**Tel**       020 7387 5006
**Opening hours**
Tues-Fri 11am – 5.30pm, Sat 11.30am – 3pm (Sat, summer only)

A welcome recent addition to the bookshops of London, they specialise in mainly secondhand and out-of-print books on art, architecture and design. There are also new books on the core topics and a nice range of periodicals and other publications.

## Boutle and King

**Address**    23 Arlington Way
London
EC1R 1UY
**Tel**    020 7278 4497
**Fax**    020 7278 4497
**Opening hours**
Mon-Fri 10.30am – 7pm, Sat 10.30am – 6pm

Started as a stall on Exmouth market and opened here in 1990, just yards from the recently re-opened Sadlers Wells Theatre and a minute or so from Angel underground. The secondhand stock is varied and interesting, especially in the areas of art, architecture, history and fiction. Other more general subjects are carried selectively but still with an emphasis on the performing arts and literature.

## Building Bookshop

**Address**    Building Centre
26 Store Street
London
WC1E 7BT
**Tel**    020 7692 4040
**Fax**    020 7636 3628
**Web**
www.buildingcentre.co.uk
**Email**
bookshop@buildingcentre.co.uk

**Opening hours**
Mon-Fri 9.30am – 5.30pm, Sat 10am – 1pm
**Services**
Mail order, catalogues, events

Located within the Building Centre (a brilliant source for building products information), the bookshop concentrates on building techniques and other related topics from architecture to town planning. DIY enthusiasts are catered for as well as students and professionals of the various trades.

## Camberwell Bookshop

**Address**    28 Camberwell Grove
Camberwell
London
SE5 8RE
**Tel**    020 7701 1839
**Fax**    020 7703 7255
**Web**
www.cambooks.demon.co.uk
**Email**
post@cambooks.demon.co.uk
**Opening hours**
Mon-Sun 11am – 7pm
**Services**
Mail order, catalogues

Situated in a quiet street of Georgian houses a short walk from Camberwell High Street and not far from the renowned art college. The stock is secondhand with a leaning towards out-of-print art and design titles. Literary and arty periodicals can also be found here. The result is a good arts bookshop with a nice range of general titles and a strong customer following.

## Chris Beetles

**Address**   10 Ryder Street
St James's
London
SW1Y 6QB
**Tel**   020 7839 7551
**Fax**   020 7839 1603
**Opening hours**
Mon-Sat 10am – 5.30pm

Don't let the 'please ring for entry' entrance put you off going inside this gallery/bookshop. The range of British watercolours is extensive – the speciality is the Victorian period – and the book stock extends to modern illustration and cartoons. Their annual 'Illustrators' exhibition is well worth looking out for and the beautifully produced show catalogues are highly sought after in their own right.

## Construction Books

**Address**   29 Leslie Park Road
Croydon
Surrey
CR0 6TN
**Tel**   020 8239 1300
**Web**
www.constructionbooks.net
**Opening hours**
Mon-Fri 9am – 6pm, Sat 10am – 2pm
**Services**
Mail order

A recent addition to the London bookselling community, the name speaks for itself in terms of the specialisation. A great source for books on all aspects of construction, architecture, design and civil engineering, for students and professionals alike.

## Design Museum Bookshop

**Address**   Butlers Wharf
Shad Thames
London
SE1 2YD
**Tel**   020 7403 6933
**Fax**   020 7378 6540
**Web**
www.designmuseum.org.uk
**Opening hours**
Mon-Sun 11am – 5.45pm
**Services**
Mail order

You can visit the shop (located on the ground floor to the left of the entrance) and enjoy a drink in the café alongside without paying for entrance to the museum proper. It's a popular spot, especially at weekends, and the shop carries a wide range of design-led products as well as a reasonable range of books.

## Dillons Arts Bookshop

**Address**   8 Long Acre
Covent garden
London
WC2E 9LH
**Tel**   020 7836 1359
**Fax**   020 7240 1267
**Opening hours**
Mon-Sat 9.30pm – 10pm, Sun noon – 6pm

Dillons is now part of the Waterstone's group and it is unclear whether this long-established arts bookshop will remain under the Dillons name, be renamed at some point in the future or perhaps relocate. In the meantime there are books on applied and fine art, at all levels and for all tastes. In addition, other general subjects are covered and the selection of art and design magazines and periodicals is particularly impressive.

# Don Kelly Books

**Address**    Antiquarius M13
135 Kings Road
London
SW3 4PW
**Tel**          020 7352 4690
**Fax**         020 7731 0482
**Opening hours**
Mon-Sat 10am – 5.30pm

Situated inside one of London's longest-established antique markets. They were founded in 1979 to provide antique collectors and dealers alike with a wide range of reference books. Apart from this shop they are also found at the Admiral Vernon Arcade, Portobello Road on Saturdays and they also exhibit at major antique fairs in London. The speciality is secondhand books on antiques, design and collectables – especially illustrated volumes.

# Dover Bookshop

**Address**    18 Earlham Street
London
WC2H 9LN
**Tel**          020 7836 2111
**Fax**         020 7836 1603
**Web**
www.thedoverbookshop.com
**Email**
images@thedoverbookshop.com
**Opening hours**
Mon-Wed 10am – 6pm, Thurs-Sat
10am – 7pm

**Services**
Mail order, catalogues

Books from the American publisher Dover constitute a huge range of craft, activity and copyright-free image source books. Many of the image collections are also available on CD Rom.

# Geffrye Museum

**Address**    Kingsland Road
London
E2 8EA
**Tel**          020 7739 5893
**Fax**         020 7729 5647
**Opening hours**
Tues-Sat 10am – 5pm

*See Museums & Galleries*

# Grays of Westminster

**Address**    40 Churchton Street
Pimlico
London
SW1V 2LP
**Tel**          020 7828 4925
020 7828 3218
**Fax**         020 7976 5783
**Opening hours**
Mon-Fri 9.30am – 5.30pm, Sat 9.30am
– 2pm

Speciality camera shop with books, manuals and expert advice on all types of Nikon cameras.

# Hayward Gallery Shop

**Address**    Hayward Gallery
South Bank Centre
Belvedere Road
London
SE1 8SX
**Tel**          020 7960 5210

*See Museums & Galleries*

## ICA Bookshop

**Address**  28 Nash House
The Mall
London
SW1Y 5AH
**Tel**  020 7925 2434
**Fax**  020 7873 0051
**Web**
www.ica.org.uk
**Email**
info@ica.org.uk
**Opening hours**
Mon-Sun noon – 9pm

Books and periodicals on art, media studies, design, women's studies, popular culture and fiction compete for space in the small bookshop off the foyer of the Institute of Contemporay Arts. There is also an enticing selection of limited edition artists books. As a non-member of the ICA it is still possible to visit the bookshop without paying to enter the exhibition galleries, cinema or café area.

## Marcus Campbell Art Books

**Address**  43 Holland Street
Bankside
London
SE1 9JR
**Tel**  020 7261 0111
**Web**
www.marcuscampbell.demon.co.uk
**Email**
campbell@marcuscampbell.demon.co.uk
**Opening hours**
Mon-Fri 10.30am – 5.30pm, Sat-Sun noon – 5pm
**Services**
Catalogues

On the ground floor of a block of Manhattan-style loft apartments overlooking the river is where you will find this secondhand bookshop specialising in modern art. Mainly dealing in books on 20th-century art there are also books on sculpture, design, architecture and photography. Marcus Campbell has been running the artists' bookfair, held at the Barbican every November, for the last seven years and consequently he also stocks an exceptional range of artists' books.

## National Gallery Bookshop

**Address**  National Gallery
Trafalgar Square
London
WC2N 5DN
**Tel**  020 7747 2870

*See Museums & Galleries*

## National Portrait Gallery

**Address**  St Martin's Place
London
WC2H 0HE
**Tel**  020 7306 0055

*See Museums & Galleries*

## Photographer's Gallery Bookshop

**Address**  5/8 Great Newport Street
London
WC2H 7HY
**Tel**  020 7831 1772
**Opening hours**

Mon-Sat 11am – 6pm, Sun noon – 6pm
**Services**
Mail order

The Photographer's Gallery was founded 25 years ago and offers one of the largest spaces devoted to photography in London. It has London's leading specialist photography bookshop with publications on every aspect of the art. You will find no difficulty in finding and enjoying books by British, American and European photographers, photo journalism, new work, landscape, architecture, history, theory and technique. The free exhibitions are worthy of note too.

## RICS Bookshop

**Address**   12 Great George Street
London
SW1P 3AD
**Tel**   020 7222 7000
**Fax**   020 7222 9430
**Web**
www.RICSbooks.org
**Opening hours**
Mon-Fri 9.30am – 5.30pm

Located at the Royal Institute of Chartered Surveyors and specialising in building, architecture, surveying, construction and property law. A catalogue is available and there is a mail order service.

## RA Bookshop

**Address**   Royal Academy of Arts
Burlington House
Piccadilly
London
W1V 0DS

**Tel**   020 7439 7438
**Fax**   020 7434 0837
**Opening hours**
Mon-Sat 10am – 5.30pm, Sun 10am – 6pm

Good range of current art books, featuring exhibition catalogues, art history and books on individual artists – plus the usual exhibition tie-ins. There is a complementary range of cards, calendars and gifts items.

## Roe and Moore

**Address**   29 Museum Street
London
WC1A 1LH
**Tel**   020 7636 4787
**Fax**   020 7636 6110
**Opening hours**
Mon-Sat 10.30am – 6pm

Found in the book enclave near the British Museum, Roe and Moore have a large collection of out-of-print and some antiquarian books on all aspects of fine art. Art of the 19th and 20th centuries predominates: on artists, exhibition catalogues, modern illustrations and reference. Modern French first editions, children's and fine bindings complete a well-rounded and appealing stock.

## Serpentine Gallery Bookshop

**Address**   Kensington Gardens
London
W2 3XA
**Tel**   020 7298 1502
**Fax**   020 7402 4103

*See Museums & Galleries*

# Shipley

**Address** 70 Charing Cross Road
London
WC2H OBB
**Tel** 020 7836 4872
**Fax** 020 7379 4358
**Web**
www.artbook.co.uk
**Email**
artbooks@compuserve.com
**Opening hours**
Mon-Sat 10am – 6pm
**Services**
Mail order, catalogues

Stands out against the mediocrity evident elsewhere on Charing Cross Road. An authoritative shop selling new, secondhand, out-of-print and antiquarian books on art and architecture, typography and graphics, photography and fashion, interior design and furniture, aesthetics, writings on art and exhibition catalogues.

# Stephen Foster

**Address** 95 Bell Street
London
NW1 6TL
**Tel** 020 7724 0876
**Fax** 020 7724 0876
**Opening hours**
Mon-Sat 10am – 6pm

A large stock of secondhand books, of which art constitutes the majority, offers something for everyone at all price levels. History and literature are also extensively stocked.

# Sims Reed Ltd

**Address** 43a Duke Street
London
SW1Y 6DD
**Tel** 020 7493 5660

*See Antiquarian*

# St James's Art Books

**Address** 15 Piccadilly Arcade
London
SW1Y 6NH
**Tel** 020 7495 6487
**Fax** 020 7495 6490
**Opening hours**
Mon-Sat 10am – 6pm

A nice shop off Piccadilly selling new, secondhand and rare books and art prints. The book stock ranges from Oriental art to the contemporary period.

# Thomas Heneage Books

**Address** 42 Duke Street
St James's
London
SW1Y 6DJ
**Tel** 020 7930 9223
**Fax** 020 7839 9223
**Email**
artbooks@heneage.com
**Opening hours**
Mon-Fri 9am – 6pm
**Services**
Catalogues

Thomas Heneage carries one of the largest range of specialist art books in the world, borne out by a superb catalogue. From interiors to Oriental art, reference to Islamic, there's little chance they won't have what you're looking for. Multi-lingual staff and a friendly atmosphere contribute to one of the best art bookshops London has to offer.

## Triangle Bookshop

**Address**     Architectural Association
               36 Bedford Square
               London
               WC1B 3EG
**Tel**         020 7631 1381
**Fax**         020 7436 4373
**Web**
www.trianglebookshop.com
**Email**
info@trianglebookshop.com
**Opening hours**
Mon-Fri 10am – 6.30pm
**Services**
Mail order, catalogues

Located in the basement of the Architectural Association, Triangle are primarily concerned with new books on architecture and landscaping with a wide-ranging choice of magazines and periodicals from the UK and abroad.

## Wallace Collection

**Address**     Hertford House
               Manchester Square
               London
               W1M 6BN
**Tel**         020 7935 0687
**Fax**         020 7224 2155

*See Museums & Galleries*

## Zwemmer at the Estorick

**Address**     The Estorick Collection
               39a Canonbury Square
               London
               N1 2AN
**Tel**         020 7704 8282
**Fax**         020 7704 8282
**Opening hours**
Wed-Sat 11am – 6pm, Sun noon – 5pm
**Services**
Mail order, catalogues

Part of the Zwemmer group, this branch opened in 1998 and is located within the Estorick gallery. On offer are books based around the collection of Italian art exhibited at this specialist gallery along with gifts imported from Italy.

## Zwemmer Art

**Address**     24 Litchfield Street
               London
               WC2H 9NJ
**Tel**         020 7379 7886
**Fax**         020 7836 7049
**Email**
zwemmer.co@btinternet.com
**Opening hours**
Mon-Fri 10am – 6.30pm, Sat 10am – 6pm
**Services**
Catalogues, mail order

A specialist of international repute and a leader in both new and out-of-print books on art. The two floors are packed with books on all aspects of the visual arts; comprehensive sections on art history, medieval art, national schools, art reference, Oriental art, 20th-century art, architecture and decorative arts are all found here. Although the stock range is extensive clear signage and helpful staff make it fairly easy to find your way around the shelves.

## Zwemmer Media

**Address**   80 Charing Cross Road
London
WC2H 9NJ
**Tel**   020 7379 7886
**Fax**   020 7836 7049
**Email**
zwemmer.co@btinternet.com
**Opening hours**
Mon-Fri 10am – 6.30pm, Sat 10am – 6pm

A sister shop to the arts emporium around the corner. Graphic design, film and photography in glorious abundance.

## Zwemmer at the Whitechapel

**Address**   Whitechapel Art Gallery
Whitechapel High Street
London
E1 7QX
**Tel**   020 7247 6924
**Opening hours**
Mon-Sun 11am – 5pm (Wed 11am – 8pm)

The concentration is firmly 20th-century art with some art reference and architecture thrown in. Special displays always back up current exhibitions providing background titles, tie-ins and catalogues. There is a good selection of magazines, cards and posters.

## Zwemmer Design

**Address**   72 Charing Cross Road
London
WC2H 0BE
**Tel**   020 7240 1559
**Opening hours**
Mon-Fri 10am – 6.30pm, Sat 10am – 6pm
**Services**
Mail order, events, catalogues, signings

The eye-catching design and layout of the shop is matched by the depth and range of stock. What can't be found in the other Zwemmer outlets can probably be unearthed here.

*Notes*

# $\mathcal{B}$usiness

**Accounting •Banking • Economics •Finance •Insurance •Law Management •Marketing •Property •Training**

## Blackwell's City Bookshop

**Address** 11 Copthall Avenue
London
EC2R 7EA
**Tel** 020 7638 1991
**Fax** 020 7638 1594
**Email**
moorgate@blackwellsbookshops.co.uk
**Opening hours**
Mon-Fri 9am – 5.30pm

Once part of Parks Bookshops, this particular Blackwell's branch is located at the office of the Institute of Chartered Accountants. Not surprisingly, the specialisation is accounting, banking, investment, company law, taxation and all related matters. There are also a few general business titles.

## Blackwell's Business and Law Bookshop

**Address** 243-244 High Holborn
London
WC1V 7DZ
**Tel** 020 7831 9501
**Fax** 020 7405 9412
**Email**
holborn@blackwellsbookshops.co.uk
**Opening hours**
Mon-Fri 9am – 5.30pm

Again, once a Parks branch but now a Blackwell's specialising in all aspects of business.

## Books etc

**Address** 54 London Wall

London
EC2M 5RA

**Tel** 020 7628 9708
**Fax** 020 7628 9643
**Opening hours**
Mon-Fri 8.30am – 6pm

Half of the shop is devoted exclusively to professional business books, in keeping with the City location: law, taxation, insurance, banking, accountancy, computing, business and management. If you can't face a visit to the West End the inter-branch ordering system will take care of anything not in stock here but available at one of the other Books etc stores.

## Chamber Bookshop

**Address** London Chamber of
Commerce
33 Queen Street
London
EC4R 1AP
**Tel** 020 7248 4444
**Fax** 020 7489 0391
**Opening hours**
Mon-Fri 9am – 5pm

A general business bookshop, with in-house Chamber publications too, aimed at Chamber of Commerce members.

## CIB City Bookshop

**Address** 90 Bishopsgate
London
EC2N 4AS
**Tel** 020 7444 7118
**Fax** 020 7444 7116
**Email**
bookorders@cib.org.uk
**Opening hours**
Mon-Fri 9am – 6pm
**Services**
Mail order, catalogues

Allied to the Chartered Institute of Bankers, this outlet has a range of books which reflects this partnership. Apart from banking and investment they also have general business books and a modest computer section.

## Dillons City Business Bookstore

**Address** 9 Moorfields
London
EC2Y 9AE
**Tel** 020 7628 7479
**Fax** 020 7251 2813
**Opening hours**
Mon-Fri 9am – 6pm

At the time of writing the only remaining Dillons campus/business bookshop with 'Dillons' above the door. Business books only here with a heavy emphasis on finance and management.

## The Economist Bookshop

**Address** 15 Regent Street
London
SW1Y
**Tel** 020 7839 1937
**Opening hours**
Mon-Fri 9am – 6pm, Sat 10am – 5pm

A pleasant shop dedicated to Economist publications and the special reports of the Economist Intelligence Unit. There are also more general business titles, particularly those with a global theme.

## Faculty Books

**Address**  Middlesex Business School
The Hendon Campus
The Burroughs
London
NW4 4BT
**Tel**  020 8202 3593

*See Academic*

## Hammicks Legal Bookshop

**Address**  191-192 Fleet Street
London
EC4A 2AH
**Tel**  020 7405 5711
**Fax**  020 7831 9849
**Email**
fleetstreet@hammicks.co.uk
**Opening hours**
Mon, Wed, Fri 9am – 6pm, Tues 9am –
6.30pm, Thurs 9am – 7pm, Sat 10am –
5pm

Impressive legal bookshop appropriately located on the corner of Chancery Lane and Fleet Street.

## James Smith

**Address**  Vicarage Field
Shopping Centre
Ripple Road
Barking
Essex
IG11 8DQ
**Tel**  020 8591 9090
**Fax**  020 8591 9937
**Email**
orders@jamesbooks.com
**Opening hours**
Mon-Sat 9am – 6pm
**Services**
Mail order, catalogues

They have a wide variety of general books in all the main subject areas stock but mainly specialise in business and computer books. The mail order business supplies customer worldwide, catalogues are issued and they are also an Open University textbooks stockist.

## Law Books Online

**Address**  29 Leslie Park Road
Croydon
Surrey
CR0 6TN
**Tel**  020 8239 1400

*See Academic*

## Law Society Shop

**Address**  113 Chancery Lane
London
WC2A
**Tel**  020 7320 5640
**Email**
marilyn.redgrave@lawsociety.org.uk
**Opening hours**
Mon-Fri 9.30am – 6.30pm
**Services**
Mail order, catalogues

A one-stop shop for all Law Society publications, books included.

## Oyez Straker

**Branch**  144-146 Fetter Lane
London
EC4 1BT
**Tel**  0870 7377370
**Web**
www.oyezstraker.co.uk
**Email**
sales.sparoad@oyez.co.uk
**Opening hours**

Mon-Fri 9am – 5pm

**Branch** 15 Artillery Row
London
SW1P 1RT
**Tel** 0870 7377370
**Web**
www.oyezstraker.co.uk
**Email**
sales.sparoad@oyez.co.uk
**Opening hours**
Mon-Fri 9am – 5pm

Formerly known as Oyez Stationery and primarily a specialist in legal and business stationery. The book stock is restricted to company matters and law only. If they don't have the legal tome you want just cross the road to Hammicks Legal.

## Stationery Office Bookshop

**Address** 123 Kingsway
London
WC2B 6PQ
**Tel** 020 7242 6393
**Fax** 020 7831 1326
**Opening hours**
Mon-Fri 9am – 5.30pm, Sat 10am – 3pm

Once known as Her Majesty's Stationery Office (HMSO) and previously located on High Holborn. The core specialisation is still Government publications – everything from the fascinating Social Trends series from the Statistical Office to White Papers. There are also more general books on business but not to the extent of those on offer at other more focused business specialists.

## Waterstone's Business Bookshop

**Address** Business Bookshop
72 Park Road
London
NW1 4SH
**Tel** 020 7723 3902
**Fax** 020 7706 1127
**Opening hours**
Mon-Fri 9.30am – 6.30pm

Once part of the Dillons empire and now under the Waterstone's banner. Located close to the London Business School business is the name of the game.

## Waterstone's

**Address** 1 Whittington Avenue
Leadenhall Market
London
EC3V 1LE
**Tel** 020 7220 7882
**Fax** 020 7220 7870

Around the corner from the Lloyds building, this branch is mainly a general bookshop but it does have a separate 'City Department' specialising in all aspects of business, particularly banking, finance, investment and general management titles.

## Wildy and Son

**Address** Lincoln's Inn Archway
Carey Street
London
WC2A 2JD
**Tel** 020 7242 5778
**Fax** 020 7430 0897
**Opening hours**
Mon-Fri 8.45am – 5.15pm

A legal atmosphere hangs in the air like a premium Havana. Situated in the picturesque Lincoln's Inn Archway, new, secondhand, antiquarian and rare books on every aspect of the law are here in abundance. The shop boasts a stock control system with details dating back over hundreds of years so product knowledge is a strong point. New books are arranged by the area of law to which they relate and a large adjacent room houses the antiquarian and secondhand range. Newspaper cuttings and other relics from famous criminal cases add to the atmosphere. If you're searching for a set of the 'Famous Trials' series you'll probably find them here – but at a price.

## Witherby & Co.

**Branch**　Book Dept
2nd floor
32-36 Aylesbury Street
London
EC1R 0ET
**Tel**　020 7251 6341
**Fax**　020 7251 1296
**Web**
www.witherbys.com

**Email**
books@witherbys.co.uk
**Opening hours**
Mon-Fri 8am – 4.30pm
**Services**
Mail order, catalogues

**Branch**　20 Aldermanbury
London
EC2V 7HY
**Tel**　020 7972 0152
**Fax**　020 7417 4431
**Opening hours**
Mon-Fri 10am – 5.30pm

Claiming to stock more insurance and shipping books than any other bookshop in the world, the roots of this business go back to 1740 when the original printing business was founded. Bookselling and publishing developed from producing books for the world of insurance in the City. The range is indeed huge and includes many imported titles. The primary motive is to supply the insurance industry both in the UK and internationally. They also supply textbooks for students taking the Chartered Insurance Institute examinations. The Aldermanbury branch opened in 1998 and is the sister shop to the Aylesbury Street store.

# Chains

**Blackwell's • Bookcase • Books etc • Borders • Dillons**
**James Thin • Ottakar's • Waterstone's • WH Smith**

## Blackwell's

Best known in Oxford for their renowned flagship store, Blackwell's made a determined move into London when they acquired a site on Charing Cross Road. They also acquired the business shops previously known as Parks Bookshops and, with the addition of two outlets at hospitals, have grown to a chain of nine bookshops in central London. Academic bookselling remains the Blackwell's strong point, as demonstrated by their internet bookshop at www.bookshop.blackwell.co.uk

**Branch** 100 Charing Cross Road
London
WC2H 0JG
**Tel** 020 7292 5100
**Fax** 020 7240 9665
**Email**
London@blackwellsbookshops.co.uk
**Opening hours**
Mon-Sat 9.30am – 8.30pm, Sun noon – 6pm

*See Academic*

**Branch** University Bookshop
158 Holloway Road
London
N7 8DD
**Tel** 020 7700 4786
**Fax** 020 7700 7687
**Email**
unl@blackwellsbookshops.co.uk
**Opening hours**
Mon-Fri 9am – 5.30pm, Sat 10am – 5pm

*See Academic*

**Branch** University of North London
Ladbroke House
62-66 Highbury Grove
London
N5 2AD
**Tel** 020 7753 5087 ext. 5193
**Opening hours**
Mon-Fri 10am – 4pm (closed 2-3)

*See Academic*

**Branch** University Bookshop
119-122 London Road
Elephant and Castle
London
SE1 6LF
**Tel** 020 7928 5378
**Fax** 020 7261 9536
**Opening hours**
Mon-Fri 9am – 6pm, Sat 10am – 5pm

*See Academic*

**Branch** South Bank University
Wandsworth Road
London
SW8 2JZ
**Tel** 020 7815 8302
**Fax** 020 7815 8302
**Email**
sbu@blackwellsbookshops.co.uk
**Opening hours**
Mon-Fri 9.30am – 5.30pm (closed 2-3)

*See Academic*

**Branch** Business and Law Bookshop
243-244 High Holborn
WC1V 7DZ
**Tel** 020 7831 9501
**Fax** 020 7405 9412
**Email**
holborn@blackwellsbookshops.co.uk

**Opening hours**
Mon-Fri 9am – 7pm
(Wed 10am – 7pm), Sat 10am – 4pm

*See Business*

**Branch** 11 Copthall Avenue
London
EC2R 7EA
**Tel** 020 7638 1991
**Fax** 020 7638 1594
**Email**
moorgate@blackwellsbookshops.co.uk
**Opening hours**
Mon-Fri 9am – 5.30pm

*See Business*

**Branch** Royal Free School
of Medicine
University of London
Rowland Hills Street
London
NW3 2PF
**Tel** 020 7830 2180
**Fax** 020 7830 2180
**Opening hours**
Mon-Fri 10am – 3pm

*See Academic*

**Branch** King's College School of
Medicine and Dentistry
Bessemer Road
London
SE5 9PJ
**Tel** 020 7346 4074
**Fax** 020 7346 4074
**Opening hours**
Mon-Fri 10am – 5pm

*See Academic*

# Bookcase

Bookcase have been operating bargain and remainder bookshops for ten years and they now have eight branches in central and inner London. They are very active in the remainder buying world and there is always something new coming into stock. The stock ranges from academic titles to current bestsellers and they also offer to take orders for full-price books. One of the branches (Waterloo Road, SE1) operates an 'obscure book of the week' recommendation which illustrates that they are slightly different from the average bargain book outlet.

**Branch**   Bookcase 2
158 Waterloo Road
London
SE1 8SB
**Tel/Fax**   020 7401 8528
**Opening hours**
Mon-Fri 9am – 7.15pm, Sat 10.30am – 6.30pm

**Branch**   Bookcase 3
268 Chiswick High Road
London
W4 4PD
**Tel/Fax**   020 8742 3919
**Opening hours**
Mon-Sat 9.30am – 7pm, Sun 11am – 5pm

**Branch**   Bookcase 4
150 Putney High Street
Putney
London
SW15 1RR
**Tel/Fax**   020 8780 1805
**Opening hours**
Mon-Sat 9am – 6pm

**Branch**   Bookcase 6
80 Victoria Street
London
SW1E 5JL
**Tel/Fax**   020 7233 5763
**Opening hours**
Mon-Fri 8.30am – 7pm, Sat 10am – 7pm

**Branch**   Bookcase 7
138-140 Charing Cross Road
London
WC2H 0LB
**Tel/Fax**   020 7836 8391/8528
**Opening hours**
Mon-Fri 9am – 8pm, Sun noon – 6pm

**Branch**   Bookcase 9
148 Charing Cross Road
London
WC2H 0LB
**Tel/Fax**   020 7836 1391
**Opening hours**
Mon-Sat 9.30am – 7.45pm, Sun noon – 5.45pm

**Branch**   Bookcase 10
97 King Street
London
W6 9JG
**Tel/Fax**   020 7741 8801
**Opening hours**
Mon-Sat 9am – 7pm, Sun 11am – 5pm

**Branch**   Bookcase 11
30-31 The Broadway
Ealing
W5 2NP
**Tel/Fax**   020 8840 7730
**Opening hours**
Mon-Sat 10am – 7pm, Sun 11am – 5pm

# Borders and Books etc

Books etc is now owned by the American bookstore giant Borders who opened their first UK superstore in Oxford Street in the summer of 1998. The only Books etc branch scheduled to be renamed Borders is the former flagship store on Chraing Cross Road – the only branch judged large enough to take the Borders treatment. In the space of 15 years Books etc has strived to become *the* bookshop chain of London and has certainly earned an enviable reputation for bookshops that are well designed, staffed by enthusiastic and knowledgeable booksellers and are great for browsing.

A differentiating factor from the other chains is that Books etc have managed to capitalise on the scale of being a chain without compromising the individual flavour of the branches. This will be tested as the Borders style influences operations but the signs are that the innovative nature of the business will not be diminished.

All the general branches offer an excellent range covering the most popular subject areas and where a shop has a genuine specialisation, this is covered in the appropriate section.

**Branch** 60 Fenchurch Street
London
EC3M 4ER
**Tel** 020 7481 4425
**Fax** 020 7702 2639
**Opening hours**
Mon-Fri 8.30am – 6.30pm

**Branch** 02 Centre
255 Finchley Road
London
NW3 6LU
**Tel** 020 7433 3299
**Fax** 020 7794 9390
**Opening hours**
Mon-Sat 10am – 10pm, Sun noon –
6pm

**Branch** 176 Fleet Street
London
EC4A 2EN
**Tel** 020 7353 5939
**Fax** 020 7583 5648
**Opening hours**
Mon-Fri 8.30am – 6.30pm

**Branch** 28 Broadway Shopping
Centre
Hammersmith
London
W6 9YY
**Tel** 020 8746 3912
**Fax** 020 8746 3676
**Opening hours**
Mon-Thurs 8am – 8pm, Fri 8am –
9pm, Sat 9am – 7pm, Sun 11am –
5.30pm

**Branch** 263 High Holborn
London
WC1V 7EE
**Tel** 020 7404 0261
**Fax** 020 7404 5187
**Opening hours**
Mon-Fri 9am – 7pm

**Branch** 54 London Wall
London
EC2M 5RA
**Tel** 020 7628 9708
**Fax** 020 7628 9643

**Opening hours**
Mon-Fri 8.30am – 6pm

*See Business*

**Branch**  421 Oxford Street
London
W1R 1FJ
**Tel**  020 7495 5850
**Fax**  020 7495 5851
**Opening hours**
Mon-Wed, Sat 9.30am – 8pm, Thurs-Fri 9.30am – 8.30pm, Sun noon – 6pm

**Branch**  23-26 Piccadilly
London
W1V 9PF
**Tel**  020 7437 7399
**Fax**  020 7437 7299
**Opening hours**
Mon-Wed, Sat 9.30am – 8pm, Thurs-Fri 9.30am – 8.30pm, Sun noon – 6pm

**Branch**  Level 2
Royal Festival Hall
South Bank Centre
London
SE1 8XX

*See Performing Arts*

**Branch**  30 Broadgate Circle
London
EC2M 2BL
**Tel**  020 7628 8944
**Fax**  020 7256 8590
**Opening hours**
Mon-Fri 8am – 8pm

**Branch**  Cabot Place East
Canary Wharf
London
E14 4QT
**Tel**  020 7513 0060
**Fax**  020 7513 0156
**Opening hours**
Mon-Fri 8.30am – 7pm, Sat 10am – 6pm

**Branch**  70-72 Cheapside
London
ECV 6EN
**Tel**  020 7236 0398
**Fax**  020 7236 0402
**Opening hours**
Mon-Fri 8.30am – 6.30pm

**Branch**  26 James Street
Covent Garden
London
WC2E 8PA
**Tel**  020 7379 6947
**Fax**  020 7497 9342
**Opening hours**
Mon-Sat 10am – 10pm, Sun noon – 6pm

**Branch**  Whitgift Centre
Croydon
Surrey
CR0 1UZ
**Tel**  020 7680 0644
**Fax**  020 7680 5958
**Opening hours**
Mon-Fri 9.30am – 6pm (Thurs 9.30am – 9pm), Sat 9am – 6.30pm, Sun 11am – 5pm

**Branch**  66 Victoria Street
London
SW1A 5LB
**Tel**  020 7931 0677
**Fax**  020 7233 5579
**Opening hours**
Mon, Thurs, Fri 8.30am – 6.30pm, Tues 9am – 6.30pm, Wed 8.30am – 7pm, Sat 9am – 6pm

**Branch**  Unit 19
Victoria Place
Victoria Station
London
SW1E 5ND
**Tel**  020 7630 6244

**Fax**    020 7233 5696
**Opening hours**
Mon-Fri 8am – 8pm, Sat 9am – 7pm,
Sun 11am – 6pm

**Branch**    Whiteleys
    Bayswater
    London
    W2 4YQ
**Tel**    020 7229 3865
**Fax**    020 7221 2393
**Opening hours**
Mon-Sat 10am – 10pm, Sun noon – 6pm

*See Children's*

**Branch**    120 Charing Cross Road

    London
    WC2H 0JR
**Tel**    020 7379 6838
**Opening hours**
Mon-Sat 9.30am – 8pm, Sun noon – 6pm

*See General*

**Borders**    197-213 Oxford Street
    London
    W1R 1AH
**Tel**    020 7292 1600
**Fax**    020 7292 1616
**Opening hours**
Mon-Sat 8am – 11pm, Sun noon – 6pm

*See General*

# Dillons

When the first edition of this guide to London's bookshops was published Dillons were second only to WH Smith in terms of the number of bookshops in and around the capital. Since Dillons came under the control of Waterstone's parent, HMV Media Group, it has been concluded that trading would cease under the Dillons name as, compared to Waterstone's, Dillons simply doesn't have a consistent and clear brand personality – even the Gower Street flagship is destined to be renamed Waterstone's.

**Branch**   82 Gower Street
London
WC1E 6EQ
**Tel**   020 7636 1577/7467 1698
**Fax**   020 7580 7680
**Opening hours**
Mon-Fri 9am – 7pm, Sat 9.30am – 6pm, Sun 11am – 5pm

*See General*

**Branch**   10-12 James Street
London
W1M 5HN
**Tel**   020 7629 8206
**Fax**   020 7495 2049
**Web**   www.dillons.co.uk
**Opening hours**
Mon-Fri 9.30am – 8pm, Sat 10am – 7.30pm, Sun noon – 6pm

**Branch**   City Business Bookstore
9 Moorfields
London
EC2Y 9AE
**Tel**   020 7628 7479
**Fax**   020 7251 2813
**Opening hours**
Mon-Fri 9am – 6pm

*See Business*

**Branch**   Wood Street
The Bentall Centre
Kingston
KT1 1TR

**Tel**   020 8974 6811
**Fax**   020 8974 6826
**Opening hours**
Mon-Fri 9.30am – 6pm, Thurs 9.30am – 8pm, Sat 9am – 6pm, Sun 11am – 5pm

**Branch**   19-23 Oxford Street
London
W1R 1RF
**Tel**   020 7434 9759
**Fax**   020 7434 3154
**Opening hours**
Mon-Fri 9.30am – 10pm, Sat 9.30am – 8pm, Sun noon – 6pm

**Branch**   8 Long Acre
Covent Garden
London
WC2E 9LH
**Tel**   020 7836 1359
**Fax**   020 7240 1267
**Opening hours**
Mon-Sat 9.30pm – 10pm, Sun noon – 6pm

*See Art & Design*

**Branch**   213 Piccadilly
London
W1V 9LD
**Tel**   020 7434 9617
**Fax**   020 7734 0681
**Opening hours**
Mon-Fri 9.30am – 10pm, Sat 9.30am – 8pm, Sun noon – 6pm

*To close in autumn 1999*

# James Thin and Volume One

James Thin is best known in Scotland but they have expanded in recent years to many medium-size towns in England, particularly through the acquisition of the Volume One chain. There are no central London branches and two of the shops (Hounslow and Ilford) will change their name from Volume One to James Thin in the near future. The four shops listed here are good general bookshops with a strong local flavour and a nice range of stock in all the most popular subject areas.

**Branch** 2a Mercer Walk
The Pavilion's
Uxbridge
Middlesex
UB8 1LY
**Tel** 01895 255969
**Fax** 01895 814110
**Opening hours**
Mon-Sat 9am – 5.30pm, Sun 10.30am – 4.30pm

**Branch** Centre Court Shopping
Wimbledon
London
SW19 8YA
**Tel** 020 8944 8879
**Fax** 020 8944 8922
**Opening hours**
Mon-Fri 9.30am – 7pm, Thurs 9.30am – 8pm, Sat 9am – 6pm, Sun 11am – 5pm

**Branch** Volume One
Treaty Centre
Hounslow
Middlesex
TW3 1ES
**Tel** 020 8569 6686
**Fax** 020 8570 0598
**Opening hours**
Mon-Fri 9.30am – 6pm, Thurs 9.30am – 7pm, Sat 9am – 6pm

**Branch** Volume One
The Exchange
Ilford
Essex
IG1 1AA
**Tel** 020 8553 5035
**Opening hours**
Mon-Sat 9.30am – 6pm, Wed 9.30am – 8pm, Sun 11am – 5pm

# Ottakar's

Ottakar's, established in 1987, is approaching 70 branches in the UK and has plans for many more. Whilst their bigger competitors have gone down the bigger-is-best route, Ottakar's have steadily and efficiently opened attractive and appealing local bookshops in towns up and down the country. Apart from the shop within the Science Museum they are not represented in central London. However, the five bookshops in Bromley, Staines, Enfield, Putney and Clapham are first-class general bookshops and always have something interesting on offer.

**Branch** Glades Shopping Centre
Bromley
Kent
BR1 1DJ
**Tel** 020 8460 6037
**Fax** 020 8460 6036
**Opening hours**
Mon-Sat 9am – 6pm, Thurs 9am –
9pm, Sun 11am – 5pm

**Branch** 77 High Street
Staines
Middlesex
TW18 4PQ
**Tel** 01784 490404
**Fax** 01784 490229
**Opening hours**
Mon-Sat 9am – 5.30pm

**Branch** 26 Church Street
Enfield
Middlesex
EN2 6BE
**Tel** 020 8363 6060
**Fax** 020 8363 6464
**Opening hours**
Mon-Fri 9am – 5.30pm, Sat 9am – 6pm

**Branch** Science Museum
Exhibition Road
South Kensington
London
SW7 2DD
**Tel** 020 7938 8255
**Fax** 020 7938 8127
**Opening hours**
Mon-Sun 10am – 6pm

*See Museums & Galleries*

**Branch** 70 St Johns Road
London
SW11 1PT
**Tel** 020 7978 5844
**Fax** 020 7978 5855
**Opening hours**
Mon-Sat 9am – 6pm, Thurs 9am –
8pm, Sun 11am – 5pm

**Branch** 6-6a Exchange Centre
Putney
London
SW15 1TW
**Tel** 020 8780 2401
**Fax** 020 8780 0861
**Opening hours**
Mon-Sat 9am – 6pm, Thurs 9am –
7pm, Sun 11am – 5pm

# Waterstone's

Having established itself as the premier literary book chain, Waterstone's is now owned by HMV Media Group, which also owns Dillons. The Dillons shops are being absorbed into the Waterstone's empire and as a result the chain now has an academic base in the London area. With 30 general bookshops in and around London (plus over ten academic or campus-based shops) you're never far from a Waterstone's branch and all they have to offer. They are also on the web at www.waterstones.co.uk

Where shops have a specific specialisation it is noted in the appropriate section of this guide. For all their general shops Waterstone's needs no introduction, they are excellent bookshops with a distinct literary feel and the new store planned to open on Piccadilly in the autumn of 1999 will be Europe's largest bookshop.

| | |
|---|---|
| **Branch** | 20-22 Market Square Bromley Kent BR1 1NA |
| **Tel** | 020 8464 6562 |
| **Fax** | 020 8466 9182 |
| **Opening hours** | |
| Mon-Sat 9am – 6pm, Thurs 9am – 8pm, Sat 11am – 5pm | |

| | |
|---|---|
| **Branch** | 128 Camden High Street London NW1 0NB |
| **Tel** | 020 7284 4948 |
| **Fax** | 020 7482 3457 |
| **Opening hours** | |
| Mon-Fri 9.30am – 8pm, Sat 9.30am – 6pm, Sun noon – 6pm | |

| | |
|---|---|
| **Branch** | 121-125 Charing Cross Road London WC2H 0EA |
| **Tel** | 020 7434 4291 |
| **Fax** | 020 7437 3319 |
| **Opening hours** | |
| Mon-Sat 9.30am – 8pm, Sun noon – 6pm | |

*See General*

| | |
|---|---|
| **Branch** | 145-147 Cheapside London EC2V 6BJ |
| **Tel** | 020 7726 6077 |
| **Fax** | 020 7726 6079 |
| **Opening hours** | |
| Mon-Fri 8am – 6.30pm | |

| | |
|---|---|
| **Branch** | 220-226 Chiswick High Road Chiswick London W4 1PD |
| **Tel** | 020 8995 3559 |
| **Fax** | 020 8995 3550 |

| | |
|---|---|
| **Branch** | 9-13 Garrick Street London WC2E 9AU |
| **Tel** | 020 7836 6757 |
| **Fax** | 020 7836 4458 |
| **Opening hours** | |
| Mon-Sat 10am – 8pm, Sun noon – 6pm | |

| | |
|---|---|
| **Branch** | Whitgift Centre Croydon Surrey CR10 1UX |
| **Tel** | 020 8686 7032 |
| **Fax** | 020 8760 0638 |

**Opening hours**
Mon-Sat 9am – 6pm, Thurs 9am –
9pm, Sun 11am – 5pm

**Branch**    64 Broadway Centre
The Broadway
Ealing
London
W5 5JY
**Tel**       020 8840 5905
**Fax**       020 8567 3246
**Opening hours**
Mon-Fri 9.30am – 7pm, Sat 9.30am –
6pm, Sun 11am – 5pm

**Branch**    266 Earl's Court Road
London
SW5 9AS
**Tel**       020 7370 1616
**Fax**       020 7244 6644
**Opening hours**
Mon-Fri 9.30am – 9pm, Sat 9.30am –
7pm, Sun noon – 6pm

**Branch**    113 High Street
Epsom
Surrey
KT19 8DT
**Tel**       01372 741713
**Fax**       01372 745636
**Opening hours**
Mon-Sat 9am – 6pm, Thurs 9am –
8pm, Sun 11am – 5pm

**Branch**    782 High Street
North Finchley
London
N12 8JY
**Tel**       020 8446 9669
**Fax**       020 8449 3663
**Opening hours**
Mon-Fri 9am – 5.30pm, Sat 9am –
6pm, Sun 11am – 4pm

**Branch**    68-69 Hampstead High Street

Hampstead
London
NW3 1QP
**Tel**       020 7794 1098
**Fax**       020 7794 7553
**Opening hours**
Mon-Fri 10am – 9pm, Sat 10am –
8pm, Sun noon – 6pm

**Branch**    Harrods
87 Brompton Road
London
SW1X 7XL
**Tel**       020 7225 5916
**Fax**       020 7225 5920
**Opening hours**
Mon, Tues, Sat 10am – 6pm, Wed-Fri
10am – 7pm

**Branch**    158-160 High Road
Ilford
Essex
IG1 1LL
**Tel**       020 8478 8428
**Fax**       020 8553 2672
**Opening hours**
Mon-Fri 9am – 7pm, Wed 9am – 6pm,
Sat 9am – 6pm, Sun 11am – 5pm

**Branch**    11 Islington Green
Islington
London
N1 2XH
**Tel**       020 7704 2280
**Fax**       020 7704 2152
**Opening hours**
Mon-Sat 9.30am – 10pm, Sun noon –
6pm

**Branch**    193 Kensington High Street
London
W8 6SH
**Tel**       020 7937 8432
**Fax**       020 7938 4970
**Opening hours**

Mon-Fri 9.30am – 9pm, Sat 9.30am –
7pm, Sun noon – 6pm

**Branch**   150-152 King's Road
Chelsea
London
SW3 3NR
**Tel**   020 7351 2023
**Fax**   020 7351 7709
**Opening hours**
Mon-Fri 9.30am – 9pm, Sat 9.30am –
8pm, Sun noon – 6pm

**Branch**   23/25 Thames Street
Kingston upon Thames
Surrey
KT1 1PH
**Tel**   020 8547 1221
**Fax**   020 8547 3071
**Opening hours**
Mon-Sat 9am – 7pm, Thurs 9am –
8pm, Sun 11am – 5pm

**Branch**   1 Whittington Avenue
Leadenhall Market
London
EC3V 1LE
**Tel**   020 7220 7882
**Fax**   020 7220 7870

*See Business*

**Branch**   39-41 Notting Hill Gate
London
W11 3JQ
**Tel**   020 7229 9444
**Fax**   020 7229 3991
**Opening hours**
Mon-Fri 9am – 8pm, Sat 9am – 7pm,
Sun noon – 6pm

**Branch**   99-101 Old Brompton Road
London
SW7 3LE
**Tel**   020 7581 8522

**Fax**   020 7225 2920
**Opening hours**
Mon-Fri 9.15am – 9pm, Sat 10.30am –
7pm, Sun noon – 6pm

**Branch**   203-206 Piccadilly
London
W1A 2AS

*See General*

**Branch**   2-6 Hill Street
Richmond
Surrey
RW10 6UA
**Tel**   020 8332 1600
**Fax**   020 8940 2595
**Opening hours**
Mon-Sat 9am – 7pm, Sun noon – 6pm

**Branch**   71-81 High Street
Sutton
Surrey
SM1 1ES
**Tel**   020 8770 0404
**Fax**   020 8643 6477
**Opening hours**
Mon-Sat 9am – 6pm, Sun 11am – 5pm

**Branch**   The Grand Building
Trafalgar Square
London
WC2N 5EJ
**Tel**   020 7839 4411
**Fax**   020 7839 1797
**Opening hours**
Mon-Sat 9.30am – 9pm, Sun noon –
6pm

**Branch**   12 Wimbledon Bridge
Wimbledon
London
SW19 7NY
**Tel**   020 8543 9899
**Fax**   020 8543 5390
**Opening hours**

Mon-Fri 9.30am – 7pm, Sat 9am – 6pm, Sun 11am – 5pm

**Branch**  Brunel University
Cleveland Road
Uxbridge
Middlesex
UB8 3PH
**Tel**  01895 257991
**Fax**  01895 232806

*See Academic*

**Branch**  City University
Northampton Square
London
EC1V 0HB
**Tel**  020 7608 0706
**Fax**  020 7251 2813

*See Academic*

**Branch**  Royal Holloway College
University of London
Egham Hill
Egham
Surrey
TW20 0EX
**Tel**  01784 471272
**Fax**  01784 431369

*See Academic*

**Branch**  Goldsmiths College
New Cross
London
SE14 6NW
**Tel**  020 8469 0262
**Fax**  020 8694 2279
**Opening hours**
Mon-Fri 9am – 7pm

*See Academic*

**Branch**  Economist Bookshop
Clare Market
Portugal Street
London

WC2A 2AB
**Tel**  020 7405 5531
**Fax**  020 7403 1584

*See Politics & Social Sciences*

**Branch**  Imperial College
Imperial College Road
London
SW7 2A2
**Tel**  020 7589 3563
**Fax**  020 7591 3810

*See Academic*

**Branch**  University Bookshop
2 Brook Street
Kingston
Surrey
KT1 2HA
**Tel**  020 8546 7592
**Fax**  020 8974 9077

*See Academic*

**Branch**  London Guildhall
University
Calcutta House
Old Castle Street
London
E1 7NT
**Tel**  020 7247 0727
**Fax**  020 7247 0513

*See Academic*

**Branch**  Business Bookshop
72 Park Road
London
NW1 4SH
**Tel**  020 7723 3902
**Fax**  020 7706 1127
**Opening hours**
Mon-Fri 9.30am – 6.30pm

*See Business*

**Branch**    Queen Mary
Westfield College
329 Mile End Road
London
E1 4NT
**Tel**        020 8980 2554
**Fax**       020 8981 6774
**Opening hours**
Mon-Fri 9am – 5.30pm

*See Academic*

**Branch**    Thames Valley University
St Mary's Road
Waling
London
W5 5RF
**Tel**        020 8840 6205
**Fax**       020 8840 6729

**Opening hours**
Mon-Fri 9am – 5pm

*See Academic*

**Hatchards**    187 Piccadilly
London
W1V 0LE
**Tel**        020 7439 9921
**Fax**       020 7494 1313

*See General*

**Mowbray's**   Waterstone's
28 Margaret Street
London
W1N
**Tel**        020 7436 0294

*See Religion & Theology*

# WH Smith

There is more on offer than meets the eye at WH Smith branches. Of course, bestsellers and only the most popular of new books tend to dominate the shelves but even the smallest branches have a reasonable range of titles across the ranges of reference, cookery, gardening, travel and paperback fiction. They operate a Clubcard scheme for customers to accumulate loyalty points and have launched a freeserve-style service to become internet service providers and presumably drive traffic to their internet bookshop.

The larger branches, such as Sloane Square, Brent Cross and Wood Green, are comprehensive general bookshops in their own right and in some areas of inner and outer London they may be the only bookshop in the vicinity. Discounts on new titles are becoming a real feature too.

Station Shop
Cannon Street
London
EC4N 6AP

16 Church Walk
Caterham
Surrey
CR3 6RT

Station Shop
Charing Cross
London
WC2N 5HS

4 Station Way
Cheam
Surrey
SM3 8SW

23 Winslade Way
Catford
London
SE6 4JU

132-138 High Street
Bromley
Kent
BR1 3EZ

Station Shop
Bromley
Kent
BR1 1LX

Brent Cross
Shopping Centre
Brent Cross
London
NW4 3FB

89 The Broadway
Bexleyheath
Kent
DA6 7JN

Station Shop
53-55 Station Parade
Barking
Essex
IG11 8TU

1 The Spires
Shopping Centre
Barnet
Herts
EN5 5XY

172 High Street
Beckenham
Kent
BR3 1EW

Ripple Walk
Vicarage Field
Barking
Essex
IG11 8DQ

370/372 Chiswick High
Road
Turnham Green
London
W4 5TA

34 North End
Croydon
Surrey
CR0 1UB

Station Shop
Croydon East Station
Surrey
CR0 1LF

125 High Street North
East Ham
London
E6 1HZ

30 Broadwalk Centre
Edgware
Middlesex
HA8 7BG

Elephant and Castle
Shopping Centre
London
SE1 6SZ

92-94 High Street
Eltham
London SE9 1BW

7-11 Palace Gardens
Shopping Centre
Enfield
Middlesex
EN2 6SN

21-23 The Broadway
Ealing
London
W5 2NH

889 Finchley Road
Golders Green
London
NW11 8RR

Kings Mall
King Street
Northside
Hammersmith
London
W6 0PZ

Station Bookshop
Fenchurch Street
London
EC3M 4AJ

Forest Hill Station
Devonshire Road
Forest Hill
London
SE23 3HD

320 North End Road
Fulham
London, SW6 1NG

St Ann's Shopping
Centre
St Ann's Road
Harrow
Middlesex
HA1 1AS

6/8 Station Road
Hayes
Middlesex
UB3 4DA

124 Holborn
Holborn Circus
London
EC1N 2TD

201-205 High Street
Hounslow
Middlesex
TW3 1BL

11 Kingsway
London
WC2B 6YA

15 Lime Street
Leadenhall Market
London
EC3M 7AA

The Bentalls Centre
Wood Street
Kingston upon Thames
Surrey
KT1 1TR

Hornton Court
132-136 Kensington
High Street
London
W8 7RP

113 Kilburn High Road
London
NW6 6JH

Station Bookshop
King's Cross
London
N1 9AP

The Bookshop
King's College Hospital
Denmark Hill
London
SE5 9RS

Ludgate Station
65 Ludgate Hill
London
EC4M 7JH

The Lewisham Centre
Lewisham
London
SE13 7EP

Liverpool Street Station
London
EC2M 7QA

Station Shop
London Bridge
London
SE1 9SP

29 Broadway
Mill Hill
London
NW7 3DA

117 Muswell Hill
Broadway
London, N10 3RS

112 High Street
New Malden
Surrey
KT3 4FU

766 High Road
North Finchley
London
N12 9QH

92 Notting Hill Gate
London
W11 3QB

189-193 High Street
Orpington
Kent
BR6 0PF

Oxford Street Plaza
London
W1N 9DP

5 Alderman's Hill
Palmers Green
London, N13 4YD

The Aylesham Centre
Rye Lane
Peckham
London
SE15 5EW

Station Parade
St Pancras
London
NW1 2QL

111-115 High Street
Putney
London
SW15 1SS

16-17 George Street
Richmond
Surrey
TW9 1JS

Station Bookshop
Richmond
Surrey
TW9 2NA

8 The Liberty
Romford
Essex
RM1 3RL

76 High Street
Ruislip
Middlesex
HA4 7AA

36 Sloane Square
London
SW1W 8AP

9-10 Harben Parade
Fincley Road
South Hampstead
London
NW3 6JS

49-51 High Street
Staines
Middlesex
TW18 4QR

41-42 The Mall
The Stratford Centre
Stratford East
London
E15 1XE

180-182 High Street
Streatham
London
SW16 1BH

Surrey Quays
Shopping Centre
Redriff Road
London
SE16 1LL

118 High Street
Sutton
Surrey
SM1 1LU

22 Temple Fortune
Parade
Temple Fortune
London
NW11 0QS

148 High Street
Uxbridge
Middlesex
UB8 1JY

Station Shop
Victoria (east)
London
SW1V 1JT

Station Shop
Victoria (island)
London
SW1V 1JT

13 High Street
Walton On Thames
Surrey
KT12 1BZ

69 Centre Mall
Arndale Centre
Wandsworth
London
SW18 4TG

Waterloo Main Station
London
SE1 7NQ

Station Shop
Waterloo Central Station
London
SE1 7NQ

64 The Broadway
West Ealing
London
W13 0SU

39-41 High Street
West Wickham
Kent
BR4 0LR

13-15 High Street
Weybridge
Surrey
KT13 8AX

82 Walm Lane
Willesden Green
London
NW2 4RA

16 Wimbledon Bridge
Wimbledon
London
SW19 7NW

110 High Road
Wood Green
London
N22 6HE

68-72 Powis Street
Woolwich
London
SE18 6LQ

# Notes

# *Children's*

**Educational • Illustrated • Multicultural • Pre-School • Teacher Resources • Teen Fiction**

## Arcade Bookshop

**Address**   3-4 The Arcade
Eltham High Street
London
SE9 1BE
**Tel**   020 8850 7803
**Fax**   020 8850 4950
**Opening hours**
Mon-Sat 9am – 5.30pm
**Services**
Mail order

Has grown steadily from a bargain outlet into a bookshop mainly dedicated to children's books. New books – many in the area of primary education – are in the majority but there are still a number of bargain books to be had in the popular subject areas. They are active in the community with regular visits to local schools and holding storytelling events in the shop.

## Bibliopola

**Address**   The Antique Market
13-25 Church Street
Marylebone
NW8
**Tel**   020 7724 7231

*See Antiquarian*

## Bookends

**Address**   1-3 Exhibition Road
South Kensington
London
SW7 2HE
**Tel**   020 7589 2285
**Opening hours**
Mon-Fri 9am – 6.30pm, Sat 10am –

6.30pm, Sun 2pm – 6pm

Located in the heart of London's Museum district and stocking a fascinating collection of books on all types of papercrafts. They have a great range of cut-out-and-make model packs from the Empire State Building to a human skeleton. The well-chosen range of children's books is equally interesting.

## Books etc

**Address**  Whiteleys
Bayswater
London
W2 4YQ
**Tel**  020 7229 3865
**Fax**  020 7221 2393
**Opening hours**
Mon-Sat 10am – 10pm, Sun noon – 6pm
**Services**
Seattle Coffee Co. and Paperchase

Although this is a general branch of the Books etc chain they have an excellent children's department with a reading area, regular storytimes and events.

## Books for Children

**Address**  97 Wandsworth Bridge Road
London, SW6 2TD
**Tel**  020 7384 1821
**Fax**  020 7736 0916
**Opening hours**
Mon 10am – 6pm, Tues-Fri 9.30am – 6pm, Sat 9.30am – 5.30pm

This bookshop prides itself on being a source of supply for many schools. The stock range is compre-hensive and covers everything from picture books for the youngest reader to educational texts.

## Bookspread

**Address**  58 Tooting Bec Road
Tooting
London
SW18 8BE
**Tel**  020 8767 6377
**Fax**  020 8767 7628
**Opening hours**
Mon, Wed, Fri 10am – 5pm, Tues, Thurs 10am – 7pm, Sat 10am – 3pm
**Services**
Events, readings

With a reputation stretching back over 20 years and knowledge to match, Bookspread have long been supplying local schools and parents with books for children. Apart from the wide-ranging stock they also have a workshop on site and arrange author visits and readings for schools and children's organisa-tions.

## Bookworm

**Address**  1177 Finchley Road
London
NW11 0AA
**Tel**  020 8201 9811
**Fax**  020 8201 9311
**Opening hours**
Mon-Sat 9.30am – 5.30pm, Sun 10am – 1pm

An imaginative shop for children and young readers. They involve their young customers in a creative way by operating a reading club with a newsletter, competitions and regular events.

## Children's Bookshop

**Address**    1 Red Lion Parade
Bridge Street
Pinner
Middlesex
HA5 3JD
**Tel**    020 8866 9116
**Fax**    020 8866 9116
**Opening hours**
Mon-Sat 9.15am – 5.30pm, Sun 10am
– 4pm
**Services**
Readings

A pleasant shop with a substantial range of books for children of all ages. They are particular active with local schools and work closely with them.

## Children's Book Centre

**Address**    237 Kensington High Street
London
W8 6SA
**Tel**    020 7937 7497
**Fax**    020 7938 4968
**Opening hours**
Mon, Wed, Thurs 9.30am – 6.30pm, Tues, Fri, Sat 9.30am – 6pm, Sun noon – 6pm
**Services**
Mail order

Founded 25 years ago, this is a bright and attractive shop arranged over two floors packed with goodies for children of all ages. The huge range is sensibly arranged by age group and subject, the staff are knowledgeable and friendly and there is also a selection of toys, computer games and learning aids on CD-ROM.

## Children's Bookshop

**Address**    29 Fortis Green Road
Muswell Hill
London
N10 3HP
**Tel**    020 8444 5500
**Fax**    020 8883 8632
**Opening hours**
Mon-Sat 9.15am – 5.45pm, Sun 11ame– 4pm (except August)
**Services**
Readings, mail order

Opposite the equally appealing Muswell Hill Bookshop and a really great bookshop for kids. Everything about the shop is geared towards children. There is a play area, toys in abundance, a regular newsletter with recommended reading suggestions, and events to keep the children interested during school holidays.

## Daisy and Tom

**Address**    181 King's Road
London
SW3 5EB
**Tel**    020 7349 5801
**Opening hours**
Mon-Fri 10am – 6pm, Wed 10am – 7pm, Sat 9.30am – 6.30pm, Sun noon – 6pm

Founded by Tim Waterstone in 1997 as part of a chain of department stores dedicated to children. A substantial part of the shop is devoted to a children's bookstore containing around 7,000 titles. There is also a daily storytime slot at 4.30pm.

## Dorling Kindersley Bookshop

**Address**  10-13 King Street
Covent Garden
London
WC2E
**Tel**  020 7836 2015
**Fax**  020 7240 1466
**Opening hours**
Mon-Fri 10am – 6pm, Sat 10.30am –
6pm, Sun noon – 6pm

There can't be many homes in middle England, or school libraries, without one of Dorling Kindersley's excellent illustrated children's reference books. Below their offices and located just off Covent Garden Piazza, you will find their full range of books including the popular eyewitness guides and a selection of multimedia products.

## Dulwich Books

**Address**  6 Croxted Road
West Dulwich
London
SE21 8SW
**Tel**  020 8670 1920
**Fax**  020 86701920
**Opening hours**
Mon-Sat 9.30am – 5.30pm
**Services**
Mail order

Primarily a general bookshop stocking all the popular subject areas but worthy of note because of its very good children's section.

## Fun Learning

**Address**  Bentall Centre
Wood Street
Kingston upon Thames
Surrey
KT1 1TP
**Tel**  020 8974 8900
**Fax**  020 8549 6612
**Email**
funlearning@dial.pipex.com
**Opening hours**
Mon-Sat 9am – 6pm, Thurs 9am –
8pm, Sun 11am – 5pm
**Services**
Mail order

Children's books, educational games, toys and software for the 5–15 age range. They also run activities during school holidays.

## Golden Treasury

**Address**  27 Replingham Road
Southfields
London
SW18 5LT
**Tel**  020 8333 0167
**Fax**  020 8874 7664
**Opening hours**
Mon-Fri 10am – 6pm, Sat 9.30am –
5.30pm

A whole range of books for children and reading for teens can be found in this friendly shop. The stock covers both fiction and educational texts along with a range of toys related to some of the more popular children's fictional characters, films and TV series.

## Harrods Children's Book Dept

**Address**  4th Floor
Harrods
Knightsbridge
London

SW1X 7XL
**Tel** 020 7225 5721
**Fax** 020 7225 5611
**Opening hours**
Mon, Tues, Sat 10am – 6pm, Wed-Fri
10am – 7pm
**Services**
Mail order, events, signings

Located separately from the general
Waterstone's bookshop in the store,
the children's department is on a
grand scale, in keeping with the rest
of Harrods. It's definitely a place
where adults come to choose books
for children as you get the distinct
feeling that kids running around
enjoying themselves among the
books might intrude on the tran-
quility. Children interested in toy
cars could also do serious damage
to the £42,000 toy Ferrari in the
nearby 'toy' department. The staff
stand out in their red waistcoats,
yellow bow ties and permanent
smiles. They are knowledgeable and
clearly willing to assist with any
enquiry. For kids keen on getting
close to the stock though, it might
be too like going to the dentist's.

## John Lewis

**Address** Brent Cross
Kingston
Oxford Street
London

**Opening hours**
Mon-Fri 10am – 8pm, Sat 9am – 6pm

Another department store that
hasn't quite struck the right note
but the children's sections are
reasonably well stocked in each

book department and may provide
a welcome break for the little ones
from shopping elsewhere in the
store.

## Kendrake Children's Bookshop

**Address** St Nicholas Centre
St Nicholas Way
Sutton
Surrey
SM1 1AY
**Tel** 020 8255 7744
**Fax** 020 8255 7744
**Opening hours**
Mon-Fri 9am – 5.30pm (Thurs 9am –
8pm), Sat 9am – 6pm, Sun 10.30am –
4.30pm
**Services**
Signings

Now in larger premises this excellent shop covers the whole range of
children's books, from pre-school,
textbooks to teenage reading. They
also have an educational section
with teacher's texts and books to
assist pressed parents and carers
with their charge's homework.

## Lion and Unicorn Bookshop

**Address** 19 King Street
Richmond
Surrey
TW9 1ND
**Tel** 020 8940 0483
**Fax** 020 8332 6133
**Opening hours**
Mon-Fri 9.30am – 5.30pm, Sat 9.30am
– 6pm
**Services**
Readings, events, mail order, signings

Jennifer Morris runs a superb and inviting shop which is a treasure trove for anyone looking for a comprehensive range of quality children's books. Subjects stocked include baby and toddler books, classics, poetry, teachers resources, parenting, children with special needs and a wide range of audio books. The staff are knowledgeable, friendly and always on hand for advice. They are also very active in putting on exhibitions, class visits and author events. Having been around for over 20 years they have established a great reputation, and the picture board behind the counter is testimony to this with joyous scenes of special events held in the shop.

## Marchpane

**Address**   16 Cecil Court
Charing Cross Road
London
WC2N 4HE
**Tel**   020 7836 8661
**Fax**   020 7497 0567
**Email**
kenneth@marchpane.demon.co.uk
**Opening hours**
Mon-Sat 10.30am – 6.30pm
**Services**
Catalogues

A box of delights in bookshop-packed Cecil Court off Charing Cross Road. The shop is located at the original site of Foyle's in 1907 and is jam packed with rare and out-of-print children's and illustrated books, which makes it a real joy to visit and browse.

## Newham Parents Centre Bookshop

**Address**   745-747 Barking Road
London
E13 9ER
**Tel**   020 8552 9993
**Fax**   020 8471 2589
**Opening hours**
Tues-Fri 9.30am – 5pm, Sat 10am – 5pm
**Services**
Events, signings

Founded 21 years ago and located near to West Ham United, this shop is everything you need in terms of a local resource. Stocking everything for the modern parent, it is particularly strong on teacher resources and all manner of children's books. General books also feature and they host regular events featuring local authors such as poet Benjamin Zephariah and Michael Rosen.

## Owl Bookshop

**Address**   209 Kentish Town Road
London
NW5 2JU
**Tel**   020 7485 7793
**Fax**   020 7267 7765
**Email**
kevinramage@eudoramail.com
**Opening hours**
Mon-Sat 9.30am – 6pm, Sun noon – 4.30pm
**Services**
Mail order

Very much a general bookshop with a good varied stock but housing an excellent children's department covering everything except school texts. The shop has a literary connection, albeit tenuous, being on the site of a department store mentioned by John Betjemen and the place where V.S. Pritchett's parents met when working in the store. The literary association continues by virtue of the numerous signed copies of books by local authors. All in all Owl is a friendly, quality local bookshop.

## Ripping Yarns

**Address**  355 Archway Road
London
N6 4EJ
**Tel**  020 8341 6111
**Fax**  020 7482 5056
**Web**
www.easyweb.easynet.co.uk/yarns
**Email**
yarns@easynet.co.uk
**Opening hours**
Mon-Fri 10.30am – 5.30pm, Sat 10am – 5pm, Sun 11am – 4pm
**Services**
Catalogues

A bookshop since the 1930s and christened Ripping Yarns in 1981 by Michael Palin and Terry Jones of Monty Python fame. Opposite Highgate tube and packed primarily with all manner of secondhand books; adventure stories, illustrated titles, some interesting annuals and old comics all seemingly jumbled together in a small space where there is precious little room to move around.

## Toys and Tales

**Address**  37 Church Street
Enfield

Middlesex
EN2 6AJ
**Tel**  020 8363 9319
**Fax**  020 8363 5053
**Opening hours**
Mon-Sat 9am – 5.30pm
**Services**
Mail order

Situated along the road from the popular local market, Toys and Tales opened in 1998 to replace the old Enfield bookshop. This pleasant shop has a good range of stock catering mainly for the up-to-teenage age group.

## Willesden Bookshop

**Address**  Willesden Green
Library Centre
95 High Road
Willesden Green
London
NW10 4QU
**Tel**  020 8451 7000
**Fax**  020 8830 1233
**Opening hours**
Mon-Fri 10am – 6pm, Sat 9.30am – 5.30pm

*See General*

## Women and Children First

**Address**  14 The Market
Greenwich
London
SE10 9HZ
**Tel**  020 8853 1296
**Opening hours**
Mon-Sun 10am – 6pm

Located in bustling Greenwich market, the name of this enterprising local bookshop says it all. It might not be able to offer the range of stock and services provided by larger children's bookshops but is a welcome respite from market shopping. The mainstay is popular reading for children of all ages and a selection of books on women's interest.

## Word Play

**Address**   1 Broadway Parade
Crouch End
London
N8 9TN
**Tel**   020 8347 6700

**Fax**   020 8347 6500
**Opening hours**
Mon-Sat 9am – 5.30pm, Sun 11am – 5pm

A great shop when you need a gift for a child but can't quite see the wisdom of shelling out a small fortune on a toy for a youngster when they'll only break it/ get bored with it/ have something like it already. There are stacks of inexpensive, pocket-money-priced goodies to keep kids happy for hours as well as a range of other toys, educational items, activity sets and a good range of children's books.

# Comics & Science Fiction

**American Cartoons • Doctor Who • Fantasy • Graphic Novels
Horror • Imports • Star Trek • Star Wars**

## Altered Images

| | |
|---|---|
| **Address** | 3 Eagle Star House |
| | 299-301 High Street |
| | Sutton |
| | Surrey |
| | SM1 1LG |
| **Tel** | 020 8770 3815 |
| **Fax** | 020 8770 3815 |

**Email**
ash.can@lineone.net

**Opening hours**
Mon-Fri 10.30am – 5.30pm (Thurs 10.30am – 7pm), Sat 9.30am – 6pm

**Services**
Mail order

Science fiction, fantasy, comics, role play and graphic posters, including imports, on the wonderful world of science fiction and fantasy.

## At the Sign of the Dragon Bookshop

| | |
|---|---|
| **Address** | 131-133 Sheen Lane |
| | East Sheen |
| | London |
| | SW14 8AE |
| **Tel** | 020 8876 3855 |
| **Fax** | 020 8876 1167 |

**Opening hours**
Mon-Sat 10am – 6pm (closed Wed)

Evocatively named general bookshop stocking new and bargain books, with a leaning towards thrillers, science fiction, fantasy and graphic novels.

## Avalon Comics

| | |
|---|---|
| **Address** | 143 Lavender Hill |
| | London |

SW11 5RA
**Tel** 020 7924 3609
**Opening hours**
Mon-Thurs 10am – 5.45pm, Fri 10am – 7pm, Sat 9.30am – 5.45pm

Comics galore, especially American, with new imports, back issues and collectors' items. Graphic novels, secondhand science fiction, horror paperbacks and associated merchandise completes the story.

## Book Palace

**Address** 81-85 Church Road
Crystal Palace
London
SE19 2TA
**Tel** 020 8768 0022
**Fax** 020 8768 0563
**Email**
david@bookpalace.com
**Opening hours**
Mon-Sat 11am – 6pm
**Services**
Mail order, catalogues

A science fiction bookshop for devotees in the south London area with the standard range of *Doctor Who*, *Star Trek* and *Star Wars* books and merchandise as well as a smattering of comics.

## Book and Comic Exchange

**Address** 14 Pembridge Road
London
W11 3HL
**Tel** 020 7229 8420
**Web**
www.buy-sell-trade.co.uk
**Email**
bookshop@bveshops.co.uk

**Opening hours**
Mon-Sun 10am – 8pm

Cheap and cheerful outlet of the Music and Video Exchange group, this particular component started life as a department in another store before eventually moving into its own premises in 1995. Barely one minute from Notting Hill Gate underground, they specialise in secondhand cult books and comics. They buy and sell anything legal and you can exchange unwanted books for vouchers or hard cash.

## Comic Shack

**Address** 720 High Road
Leytonstone
London
E11 3NN
**Tel** 020 8539 7260
**Web**
www.comicshack.uk.com
**Email**
comic.shock@dialpipex.com
**Opening hours**
Mon-Sat 9.30am – 5.30pm, Sun 11am – 5pm
**Services**
Mail order

American comics is the main specialisation with science fiction and fantasy paperbacks as a sideline. The prices range from as low as 50p to a staggering £2,500 for the rarest comics on offer.

## Comic Showcase

**Address** 63 Charing Cross Road
London
WC2H
**Tel** 020 7240 3664

**Opening hours**
Mon-Wed 10am – 6pm, Thurs, Fri
10am – 7pm, Sat 9.30am – 7pm, Sun
10am – 6pm

Originally on Neal Street in Covent
Garden but recently moved to this
bright new shop just down from
Murder One, the crime and thrillers
bookshop. They have a substantial
range of comics, mainly American,
and associated merchandise in
keeping with the genre.

## Fantasy Centre

**Address**   157 Holloway Road
London
N7 8LX
**Tel**   020 7607 9433
**Opening hours**
Mon-Sat 10am – 6pm

Mainly secondhand books here in
the fields of science fiction, fantasy
and horror and there is a small
section of first editions and a few
new books. The Fantasy Centre has
been around for 20 years, unlike
many of the comic-oriented
newcomers, so the stock and
services are more complete than
some other outlets. The paperbacks
(especially the older ones with
surreal cover illustrations), magazines and ephemera are generally
better than average. Subject catalogues are issued regularly.

## Forbidden Planet

**Address**   71-75 New Oxford Street
London
WC1A
**Tel**   020 7836 4179

**Opening hours**
Mon-Wed, Sat 10am – 6pm, Thurs, Fri
10am – 7pm
**Services**
Events, signings

Forbidden Planet is the undisputed
leader in this field. The London
shop occupies two floors and has
three separate departments. The
range of books on science fiction,
fantasy and horror includes many
hard-to-get imports and is the most
comprehensive anywhere. Comics
new, old and rare come from all
over the world as does the bewilder-
ing range of related merchandise.
Rare items are kept behind the
counters, where expert advice from
fellow fanatics is always to hand.
Uniquely there is a special section
for Small Press publications.
Limited and signed editions are
available along with an intriguing
selection of TV fantasy stuff
(notable *Buffy The Vampire Slayer*)
and film books.

## Gosh! Comics

**Address**   39 Great Russell Street
London
WC1B 3PH
**Tel**   020 7636 1011
**Fax**   020 7436 5053
**Opening hours**
Mon-Sun 10am – 6pm (Thurs, Fri
10am – 7pm)
**Services**
Mail order

Opened in 1986 as a pure comic
shop, it has since been expanded by
Josh Palmanos in an imaginative
way into newspaper strip art and

has the largest collection in the UK. As well as selling compilation books they also sell original art work of cartoon favourites such as Steve Bell. The book and comic stock is mainly new and ranges from obscure American editions to old favourites such as beautifully illustrated Barbar books to good old Doctor Seuss.

## Magpie Bookshop

**Branch**    53 Brushfield Street
Spitalfields
London
E1 6AA
**Tel**    020 7247 4263

**Branch**    The Clerks House
118 Shoreditch High Street
London
E1
**Tel**    020 7729 5076

*See Secondhand*

## Mega-City Comics

**Address**    18 Inverness Street
London
NW1 7HJ
**Tel**    020 7485 9320
**Fax**    020 7428 0700
**Email**
megacity@compuserve. com
**Opening hours**
Mon-Wed, Sat, Sun 10am – 6pm, Thurs, Fri 10am – 7pm
**Services**
Mail order, catalogues

Opened in 1987, this shop is now one of the biggest stockists of American comics in the UK. With supposedly 250,000 comics in stock and a worldwide mail order service available to those who can't visit, this is the place to go for your comic needs.

## Skinny Melinks

**Address**    66 Loampit Vale
Lewisham
London
SE13
**Tel**    020 8318 0499
**Opening hours**
Mon-Wed 11am – 6pm, Thurs, Fri 11am – 7pm, Sat 1pm – 6pm, Sun 11am – 5pm

Worth visiting for the name alone, this streetwise comic and graphic novel shop sells mainly new comics with a decent range of secondhand and collector's issues.

## Tintin Shop

**Address**    34 Floral Street
London
WC2E
**Tel**    020 7536 1131
**Opening hours**
Mon-Sat 10am – 6pm
**Services**
Mail order

Blistering Barnacles! For the last 15 years the Tintin shop has specialised in books by Herge and products derived from his artwork and characters. If the books don't appeal, the goods based on them will: clothing, cards, prints, watches, calendars, diaries, models and jigsaws to name but a few of the products branded with the ginger-quiffed hero's name.

## Who Shop

**Address**   4 Station Parade
            High Street North
            London
            E6
**Tel**       020 8471 2356
**Opening hours**
Mon-Sat 9.30am – 5.30pm

*Doctor Who* fanatics are catered for in every conceivable way in this east London mecca for followers of the most noble of time travellers. Books and videos dominate along with a host of *Doctor Who* toys, collectables and other such things. There are also books and videos based on other popular TV science fiction and fantasy series such as *Red Dwarf* and *Babylon 5*.

# Notes

# Computing

**Apple Macs • Computer Aided Design • Internet •PCs
Programming • Web Site Creation**

## James Smith

| | |
|---|---|
| **Address** | Vicarage Field Shopping Centre Ripple Road Barking Essex IG11 8DQ |
| **Tel** | 020 8591 9090 |

*See Business*

## Mega-Byte Books

| | |
|---|---|
| **Branch** | 18-19 Aldgate Barrs Shopping Centre Gardeners Corner London E1 7PJ |
| **Tel** | 020 7481 2651 |
| **Fax** | 020 7481 2652 |
| **Web** | www.megabytebook.co.uk |
| **Email** | info@.megabytebook.co.uk |
| **Opening hours** | Mon-Fri 10am – 6pm |
| **Services** | Mail order |
| **Branch** | 15-17 Colonnade Walk 125 Buckingham Palace Road London, SW1W |
| **Tel** | 020 7828 8412 |
| **Fax** | 020 7481 2652 |

This dedicated computer book specialist serves the City and beyond with these two branches. Not only do they have a huge range of books on every aspect of computing, many titles are discounted too.

## PC Bookshop

**Branch**　21 Sicilian Avenue
Southampton Row
London
WC1A 2QH
**Tel**　020 7831 0022
**Fax**　020 7831 0443
**Web**
www.pcbooks.co.uk
**Email**
orders@pcbooks.demon
**Opening hours**
Mon-Fri 9.30am – 6pm (Thurs 9.30am – 7pm), Sat 10.30am – 5.30pm
**Services**
Mail order, catalogues, events

**Branch**　34 Royal Exchange
Threadneedle Street
London
EC3V 3LP

**Tel**　020 7621 0888
**Fax**　020 7621 0999
**Opening hours**
Mon-Fri 8.30am – 6pm

The Sicilian Arcade branch is housed in a Grade 2 listed shopping arcade. PC Bookshop was founded in 1991 and became one of the first specialist computer bookshops in London. They have grown from one shop to occupy the unit next door in Sicilian Arcade and have also opened a site in the heart of the City's financial district. The staff have expert knowledge and can cater for the complete beginner and IT professional alike.

# *Countries*

**Africa • Asia • Australia • Eastern Europe • France • Greece • Ireland Italy • Japan • Middle East • New Zealand • Spain •Tibet**

## Africa Book Centre

**Address** 38 King Street
London
WC2E 8JT
**Tel** 020 7240 6649
**Fax** 020 7497 0309
**Email**
africabooks@dial.pipex.com
**Opening hours**
Mon-Fri 10am – 6pm (Thurs 10am – 7pm)
**Services**
Review list

Visit the Africa Centre to see the paintings and crafts in the ground-floor gallery and head upstairs for the bookshop. There is a wide range of books on all subjects relating to Africa, black America, the Caribbean and Third World development. Literature, art, languages, travel, music, history, politics, social studies, education and children's are the main subjects. Records, cassettes, cards and T-shirts are also available.

## Alkitab Bookshop

**Address** 128c London Road
Kingston upon Thames
Surrey
KT2 6QJ
**Tel** 020 8549 4479
**Fax** 020 8549 4479
**Opening hours**
Mon-Sat 10.30am – 6pm
**Services**
Mail order

Books on the Middle East are to be found here, primarily in Arabic, covering the main subject areas of history, travel and art. They also stock some English translations.

# Al Saqi Books

**Address**   26 Westbourne Grove
London
W2 5RH
**Tel**   020 7229 8543
**Fax**   020 7229 7492
**Web**
alsaqibooks@compuserve.com
**Opening hours**
Mon-Sat 10am – 6pm
**Services**
Mail order, catalogues

Housed in the Kufa Gallery which promotes Oriental arts and culture. They have a range of books in English on the Middle East as well as books in Arabic from Lebanon, Egypt and most of the Arab countries.

# Al-Hoda

**Address**   76 Charing Cross Road
London
WC2H OBB
**Tel**   020 7240 8381
**Opening hours**
Mon-Sat 10am – 6pm

The range of books in Al Hoda is divided into three main areas governed by language: English, Arabic and Persian and Urdu. The subject range is akin to that in a general bookshop, with an emphasis on language learning materials and topics of popular relevance to the Middle East. Most of the stock is new but there are also some out-of-print and secondhand books.

# Al-Noor Bookshop

**Address**   82 Park Road
London
NW1 4SH
**Tel**   020 7723 5414
**Fax**   020 7723 5414
**Opening hours**
Mon-Sat 10am – 7pm

Specialises in books on Islam and the Middle East, in both English and Arabic.

# Anthony C Hall

**Address**   30 Staines Road
Twickenham
TW2 5AH
**Tel**   020 8898 2638
**Fax**   020 8893 8855
**Web**
achallbooks@intonet.co.uk
**Opening hours**
Mon-Fri 9am – 5.30pm

Secondhand and some antiquarian books on Russia and her neighbours in Asia, Eastern Europe and the Middle East.

# Arthur Probsthain

**Address**   41 Great Russell Street
London
WC1 3PL
**Tel**   020 7636 1096
**Fax**   020 7636 1096
**Opening hours**
Mon-Fri 9.30am – 5.30pm, Sat 11am – 4pm
**Services**
Mail order, catalogues

Family run since 1903, Arthur Probsthain specialise in new, antiquarian and secondhand books on all Oriental and African topics. They are the leaders in their field and therefore the stock range is more comprehensive than anywhere else in town. Regular catalogues are issued to make it easier for customers to keep up to date with recently published and forthcoming titles in their area of interest.

## Asian Bookshop

**Address**  112 Whitfield Street
London
W1P 5RU
**Tel**  020 7387 5747
**Fax**  020 7388 2662
**Email**
asianbooks@aol.com
**Opening hours**
Mon-Sat 11am – 6pm
**Services**
Mail order, catalogues

On the corner of Whitfield Street and Grafton Way, this bookshop deals extensively in anything and everything to do with Asia. The range of stock covers most subjects from art to travel in the languages of the region: Hindu, Urdu, Bengali, Gujerati and Punjabi. As well as a fine selection of books they also stock a good range of Indian films and music.

## Australian Shop

**Address**  26 Henrietta Street
Covent Garden
London
WC2E 8NA
**Tel**  020 7836 2292
**Fax**  020 7385 7253
**Web**

www.australiashop.co.uk
**Email**
austshop@dircon.co.uk
**Opening hours**
Mon-Sat 10.30am – 6.30pm, Sun 11am – 5.30pm

Previously located at Western Australia House on the Strand and a sister shop to the Australian Bookshop in Woburn Walk. These two outlets have now merged to become the Covent Garden-based Australian Shop. There are plenty of Antipodean souvenirs available along with a choice of guide books, maps and a nice range of illustrated books on the natural beauty of the Antipodes.

## Books Nippon

**Address**  64-66 St Paul's Churchyard
London
EC4M 8AA
**Tel**  020 7248 4956
**Opening hours**
Mon-Fri 10am – 7pm, Sat 10am – 6pm

Books about and from Japan in Japanese and in English translation. There are also Japanese news-papers, magazines, comics, cards and many other everyday and gift items in what must be home from home for Japanese visitors to London.

## Dar Al Dawa

**Address**  97 Westbourne Grove
Bayswater
London, W2
**Tel**  020 7221 6256
**Opening hours**

Mon-Sun 9am – 10pm

Islamic and Middle Eastern history are the features of this predominantly Arabic language bookstore. However, the language and reference section has a small selection of titles in English.

## Eastern Books

**Address**   81 Replingham Road
              Southfields
              London
              SW18 5LU
**Tel**       020 8871 0880
**Fax**       020 8871 0880
**Web**
www.easternbooks.com
**Email**
info@easternbooks.com
**Opening hours**
Mon-Sun noon – 7pm
**Services**
Mail order, catalogues, online ordering

Founded originally as a mail order company, they now have their own shop in Southfields. Specialising in rare and antiquarian books on the Orient, Middle East and Africa, they have over ten years of experience in this field and claim to have one of the most complete ranges available in Europe.

## Fine Books Oriental

**Address**   38 Museum Street
              London
              WC1A 1LP
**Tel**       020 7242 5288
**Fax**       020 7242 5344
**Web**
www.finebooks.demon.uk
**Email**

oriental@finebooks.demon.co.uk
**Opening hours**
Mon-Sat 9.30am – 5.30pm
**Services**
Mail order, catalogues

Antiquarian and secondhand stock specialising in Japan, the Far East and Asia. Photographs and postcards complement the range of books.

## Four Provinces Bookshop

**Address**   244 Grays Inn Road
              London
              WC1X
**Tel**       020 7833 3022
**Opening hours**
Tues-Sat 11am – 4pm

New and secondhand books on Ireland and Irish culture covering all the popular main subject areas. Naturally, there is a good selection of Gaelic titles along with Irish music on tape. The shop also provides a valuable service as an information distribution point for all manner of Irish events throughout London.

## French Bookseller Librairie La Page

**Address**   7 Harrington Road
              South Kensington
              London
              SW7 3ES
**Tel**       020 7589 5991
**Fax**       020 7225 2662
**Opening hours**
Mon-Fri 8.20am – 6.15pm, Sat 10am – 5pm

**Services**

Mail order, catalogues

One of two excellent French bookshops in London with the added advantage that they are not far apart. In addition to the wide range of books are cards, stationery products, magazines and videos.

# French Bookshop

**Address**  28 Bute Street
South Kensington
London
SW7
**Tel**  020 7584 2840
**Opening hours**
Mon-Fri 8.30am – 6pm, Sat 10am – 5pm

Students from the nearby Lycee use this well-stocked bookshop for reference books, French bilingual books, paperback fiction and graphic novels. French literature is the focus among the large number of titles and children's books are also well represented. French games and stationery are also available. A selection of French newspapers and periodicals add to the Gallic flavour.

# Greek Bookshop (Zeno)

**Address**  6 Denmark Street
London
WC2H 8LP
**Tel**  020 7240 1968
**Fax**  020 7836 2522
**Web**
www.thegreekbookshop.com
**Email**
info@thegreekbookshop.com
**Opening hours**
Mon-Fri 9.30am – 6pm, Sat 9.30am – 5pm

**Services**

Mail order, catalogues

Located just off Charing Cross Road, the Greek Bookshop was established by Father Kykkotis, a monk from the Cyprus Monastery of Kykko, during the Second World War. He set out to provide Greeks and Cypriots in London with books in Greek and English about Greece, Cyprus, the Ottoman Empire and the Balkans. The tradition he established continues today.

# Grenville Books

**Address**  40a Museum Street
London
WC1A 1LT
**Tel**  020 7404 2872
**Fax**  020 7404 2872

*See Secondhand*

# Guanghwa Co. Ltd

**Address**  7 Newport Place
London
WC2H 7JR
**Tel**  020 7437 3737
**Fax**  020 7831 0137
**Opening hours**
Mon-Sat 10.30am – 7pm, Sun 11am – 7pm
**Services**
Mail order

Two floors of books in Chinese across a wide range of subjects including a good selection of language learning materials and books in English on Chinese topics. Additionally, the section of Chinese art materials is more comprehensive than the average graphic arts shop.

## Han-Shan Tang Books

**Address**  Unit 3 Ashburton Centre
276 Cortis Road
London
SW15 3AY
**Tel**  020 8788 4464
**Fax**  020 8780 1565
**Web**
www.hanshan.com
**Email**
hst@hanshan.com
**Opening hours**
Mon-Fri 10am – 5.30pm, by
appointment
**Services**
Mail order, catalogues

Founded in 1978, Han-Shan
describes itself as the West's foremost book dealer specialising in the
art of Asia. They do not have a
retail shop but appointments are
welcome to peruse the stock of this
highly specialised dealer.

## Hellenic Book Service

**Address**  91 Fortess Road
Kentish Town
London
NW5 1AG
**Tel**  020 7267 9499
**Fax**  020 7267 9498
**Web**
www.hellenicbookservice.com
**Email**
hellenicbooks@btinternet.com
**Opening hours**
Mon-Fri 9.30am – 6pm, Sat 10am –
5pm
**Services**
Mail order

Founded in 1966 and originally
situated in Charing Cross Road,
Hellenic moved to Kentish Town in

1991 and competes with Zeno to be
the biggest Greek bookshop outside
Greece or Cyprus. New books form
the bulk of the stock but there are
plenty of secondhand books too.

## Hosains Books

**Address**  25 Connaught Street
London
W2 2AY
**Tel**  020 7262 7900
**Fax**  020 7794 7127
**Opening hours**
By appointment
**Services**
Catalogues, book search

An antiquarian bookseller specialising in Central Asia, South Asia and
the Middle East. Subjects represented include religion, travel and
history. Part of the magic is
provided by a fine range of mini-
atures, lithographs and manuscripts
relating to the specialisation.

## Green Ink Books

**Address**  8 Archway Mall
London
N19 5RG
**Tel/Fax**  020 7263 4748
**Opening hours**
Mon-Sat 10am – 6pm
**Services**
Mail order, events, readings, signings

A tatty cardboard notice attached
to a concrete bollard outside
Archway post office points the way
to this Irish bookshop. The location, in the tatty precinct by
Archway underground station, may
be unpromising but the bookshop is
welcoming and stocks a wide range

of books on Ireland. They also have a range of CDs, videos and cassettes.

## Italian Bookshop

**Address**   7 Cecil Court
Charing Cross Road
London
WC2N 4EZ
**Tel**   020 7240 1634
**Fax**   020 7240 1635
**Email**
italianbookshop@freenet.co.uk
**Opening hours**
Tues-Sat 10.30am – 6.30pm
**Services**
Mail order, events, catalogues

Owned by the Messaggerie Libra Spa, the largest book distributor in Italy, they offer a good range of books in Italian and in English translation. Italian literature, art, travel guides, language learning, reference titles and children's books complete the stock. Italian films on video and magazines are also available.

## Japan Centre

**Address**   212 Piccadilly
London
WIV 9LD
**Tel**   020 7439 8035
**Opening hours**
Mon-Sat 10am – 8pm, Sun 10am – 6pm

The basement is devoted to Japanese foods and the two floors above to books, magazines and newspapers on every aspect of Japan and Japanese culture – in English and in Japanese. A huge selection of Japanese novels are available along with graphic novels and comics. The selection of language learning materials is equally comprehensive.

## John Randall Books

**Address**   47 Moreton Street
London
SW1V 2NY
**Tel**   020 7630 5331
**Opening hours**
By appointment only

Not a bookshop but nonetheless a fine range of books on Asia are available from this specialist dealer. Primarily antiquarian, rare and secondhand but with some new books as well.

## Kilburn Bookshop

**Address**   8 Kilburn Bridge
Kilburn High Road
London
NW6 6HT
**Tel**   020 7328 7071
**Fax**   020 7372 6474
**Opening hours**
Mon-Sat 10am – 6pm

*See Politics & Social Sciences*

## Lloyd's of Kew

**Address**   9 Mortlake Terrace
Kew
London
TW9 3DT
**Tel**   020 8940 2512

*See Crafts & Pastimes*

## Maghreb Bookshop

**Address**  45 Burton Street
London
WC1H 9AL
**Tel**  020 7388 1840
**Opening hours**
By appointment

The Maghreb countries of North Africa comprise Algeria, Libya, Mauritania, Morocco and Tunisia. Books covering academic studies and Islam are available in Arabic and French and the shop prides itself on having a definitive collection of books in their field.

## Neal Street East

**Address**  5 Neal Street
Covent Garden
London
WC2H 9PU
**Tel**  020 7240 0135
**Opening hours**
Mon-Sat 11am – 7pm, Sun noon – 6pm

Located in an old Covent Garden vegetable warehouse, this is a shop that specialises in crafts and products from the Far East, South-East Asia and the Indian subcontinent. Ilustrated books are a strong point along with books on Chinese and Japanese art techniques.

## New Beacon Books

**Address**  76 Stroud Green Road
London
N4 3EN
**Tel**  020 7272 4889
**Fax**  020 7281 4662
**Opening hours**
Mon-Sat 10.30am – 6pm

**Services**
Catalogues

An impressive range of books on black Britain, the Caribbean, Africa and black America on subjects from cookery to radical politics. Within the multicultural section are many children's books you may find hard to find in most general bookshops.

## New Zealand Kiwi Fruits

**Address**  7 Royal Opera Arcade
Pall Mall
London
SW1Y 4UY
**Tel**  020 7930 4587
**Fax**  020 7839 0592
**Opening hours**
Mon-Fri 9am – 5.30pm, Sat 10am – 4pm
**Services**
Mail order

A small shop located in the Royal Opera Arcade behind Her Majesty's Theatre on Haymarket. Full of New Zealand gifts and souvenirs, there is room left over for a great range of books and magazines from and about New Zealand. The range goes beyond travel guides and popular fiction to include natural history, the Maori language and people, and children's books.

## OCS Japanese Books

**Address**  2 Grosvenor Parade
Uxbridge Road
Ealing
London
W5 3NN
**Tel**  020 8992 6335

**Fax**    020 8993 0891
**Opening hours**
Tues-Sat 10am – 6pm

Originally located in Camden next
to the Japanese school, they moved
with the school to Ealing in 1987.
They provide books in Japanese
and English on Japanese subjects
and give discounts to Japanese
language students on textbooks.

## O'Flanagans Irish Bookshop

**Address**    81 Westbourne Park Road
    London
    W2 5QH
**Tel**    020 7229 3626
**Fax**    020 7229 3626
**Web**
www.oflanagans.com
**Email**
info@oflanagans.com
**Opening hours**
Tues-Sat 10am – 6pm
**Services**
Mail order, signings, catalogues, events

Opened in 1997, this third Irish
bookshop in London stocks new,
out-of-print and antiquarian books
of Irish interest. The shop features
the glass work of artist Stephanie
Cartton and has the advantage of a
garden in which customers can
relax in the summer.

## Orbis Books

**Address**    66 Kenway Road
    Earl's Court
    London
    SW5 0RD
**Tel**    020 7370 2210
**Fax**    020 7742 7686

**Email**
bookshop@orbis-books.co.uk
**Opening hours**
Mon-Fri 10am – 5.30pm, Sat 10am –
4.30pm
**Services**
Mail order, catalogues

Originally established in 1944 to
serve the Polish Army stationed in
England after the war. They have a
wide range of books in English on
Eastern Europe as well as books in
Polish, Czech and Slovak. There are
also Polish newspapers (one
published in England) and a
selection of magazines.

## PMS Bookshop

**Address**    240 King Street
    London
    W6 0RF
**Tel**    020 8748 5522
**Fax**    020 8748 5522
**Opening hours**
Mon-Sat 10am – 6pm (Fri 10am – 7pm)

This dedicated bookshop within the
Polish Centre in Hammersmith
stocks all things Polish. The books
in Polish include education, history,
literature, politics and culture and
there is plenty of choice of books
and cassettes in English and Polish
for those learning the language.
Souvenirs from Poland, toys, flags
and other merchandise accompany
Polish daily newspapers, calendars
and magazines. This is a cultural
centre and a reference point for the
Polish community in and around
London, in which the bookshop is a
focal point.

## Rowland Wards Holland and Holland

**Address**   Holland and Holland
31-33 Bruton Street
London
W1X 8JB
**Tel**   020 7499 4411
**Fax**   020 7499 4544
**Opening hours**
Mon-Fri 9.30am – 5.30pm

Tucked away among the guns, shooting accessories and outdoor clothing for the hunting and fishing set, is a bookshop unique in London. Books on field sports, hunting, fishing, safaris and travel guides are available along with an enticing selection of illustrated volumes on Africa. Some sort of balance is achieved by a number of books on conservation management.

## Soma Books

**Address**   38 Kennington Lane
London
SE11 4LS
**Tel**   020 7735 2101
**Fax**   020 7735 3076
**Web**
www.somabooks.co.uk
**Email**
books@somabooks.co.uk
**Opening hours**
Mon-Fri 9.30am – 5.30pm, Sat 10am – 4pm
**Services**
Mail order, catalogues

A substantial range of books on Africa, the Caribbean, black America and associated issues of race and education. General subjects are also covered and the children's section stands out with an innovative and carefully chosen range of multicultural, anti-sexist and anti-racist books. Crafts, posters and cards include many items of interest imported from Asia.

## Tibet Shop

**Address**   10 Bloomsbury Way
London
WC1A 2SH
**Tel**   020 7405 5284
**Fax**   020 7404 2336
**Opening hours**
Mon-Sat 10am – 6pm

The Tibet shop provides a wide range of traditional arts and crafts, and books based on Tibetan Buddhism and culture.

## Ying Hwa

**Address**   14 Gerrard Street
London
W1V
**Tel**   020 7439 8825
**Opening hours**
Mon-Sun 11am – 7.30pm

Mainly Chinese books and magazines for the workers and residents of London's Chinatown.

# *Crafts & Pastimes*

**Bookbinding • Calligraphy • Ceramics • Chess • Cookery • Crafts
Fashion • Gambling • Gardening • Magic • Numismatics • Philately**

## Bookends

**Address**  1-3 Exhibition Road
South Kensington
London
SW7 2HE
**Tel**  020 7589 2285

*See Children's*

## Books for Cooks

**Address**  4 Blenheim Crescent
Notting Hill
London
W11 1NN
**Tel**  020 7221 1992
**Fax**  020 7221 1517
**Web**
www.booksforcooks.com
**Email**
info@booksforcooks.com
**Opening hours**

Mon-Sat 9.30am – 6pm
**Services**
Events, signings, mail order, catalogues

The smell of food is the first thing that hits you when you walk in what is one of the best specialist bookshops in London. The innovative Books for Cooks has been a feature of London's book and culinary world for over 16 years and has become a central reference point for foodies and chefs alike. They have a demonstration kitchen at the back of the shop where you can indulge in a three-course lunch for around £10, with menus and chefs changing daily. The cookery school was started a few years ago and has proved to be another success. Apart from all this they have what is probably the most comprehensive range of cookery books in the world and expert staff to go with it. One day they will have to move to larger premises but until then, do not miss this shop.

## Booktree

| | |
|---|---|
| **Address** | Merton Abbey Mills |
| | Merantun Way |
| | South Wimbledon |
| | London |
| | SW19 2RD |
| **Tel** | 020 8540 2694 |
| **Fax** | 020 8543 0792 |

**Opening hours**
Mon-Sun 10am – 5pm
**Services**
Mail order, catalogues

A visit to the South London Craft Village yields a variety of attractions and is a pleasant way to spend a slow Sunday. The Mill was once a printing works and the waterwheel is one of few still operating. Booktree specialises in books on handcrafts: woodwork, embroidery, papercrafts, floristry and drawing techniques along with all the products and materials you'll need to get started. The craft market sells ethnic food and home-made goods on weekends and holidays.

## British Library Bookshop

| | |
|---|---|
| **Address** | 96 Euston Road |
| | London |
| | NW1 2DB |
| **Tel** | 020 7412 7735 |
| **Fax** | 020 7412 7172 |
| **Email** | bl-bookshop@bl.uk |

**Opening hours**
Mon-Fri 9.30am – 6pm (Tue 9.30am – 8pm), Sat 9.30am – 5pm
**Services**
Mail order, events, signings, readings

Contained in the new British Library complex opposite St Pancras station, this fine shop is a bibliophile's dream. There are books on books, manuscripts, bookbinding, papermaking, printing, illustration and calligraphy. There are also other books on art, history, reference and on London itself. The gift products include many quality items and as well as the cards and posters you will find handmade paper and quill pens.

## Chess and Bridge

| | |
|---|---|
| **Address** | 369 Euston Road |
| | London |
| | NW1 3AR |
| **Tel** | 020 7388 2404 |

**Opening hours**
Mon-Sat 10am – 6pm

Chess and bridge enthusiasts will probably already know of this specialist on the Euston Road between Warren Street and Great Portland Street underground stations. Beginners and advanced players are welcome to inspect the wide selection of books solely devoted to chess and bridge. There is a good range of associated merchandise such as computer chess games, software and card tables. The service from the staff is enthusiastic and knowledgeable and book lists are available.

## Contemporary Ceramics

**Address**   William Blake House
7 Marshall Street
London
W1V 1LP
**Tel**   020 7437 7605
**Opening hours**
Mon-Sat 10am – 5.30pm, Thurs 10am – 7pm

The retail outlet for members of the Craft Potters Association has been selling the work of the finest potters and ceramists in Britain since 1960. Books on the craft sit alongside tools, equipment and displays of ceramics.

## Davenport's Magic Shop

**Address**   7 Charing Cross
Underground Arcade
The Strand
London
WC2N 4HZ
**Tel**   020 7836 0408
**Fax**   020 7379 8828
**Opening hours**
Mon-Sat 9.30am – 5.30pm
**Services**   Mail order, catalogues

Having just celebrated its centenary and long may they continue to be one of the oddities of the London book scene. You may need telepathic powers to find your way to this shop tucked away in the bowels of Charing Cross station, but once there you will be entranced by a shop entirely devoted to the world of magic and conjuring. Mystical apparatus and equipment domi-nates the shop but there are books on white magic, conjuring, ventrilo-quism and mind-reading. A studio accommodates regular talks and demonstrations from famous expo-nents of magic tricks and creators of illusion. The London Society of Magicians meets here every fort-night and new members are always welcome. If you can't make regular visits do what lots of other customers do and use the mail order service – a charge is made for the catalogue.

## Embroiderers' Guild Bookshop

**Address**   Apartment 41
Hampton Court Palace
East Molesey
Surrey
KT8 9AU
**Tel**   020 8943 1229
**Fax**   020 8977 9882
**Email**
lenglish@embroidersguild.org.uk
**Opening hours**
Mon-Fri 10am – 4pm
**Services**
Book lists

The bookshop is found in the splen-dour of Hampton Court Palace so once you've found your way out of the famous maze, you'll discover a plethora of books on all aspects of embroidery for everyone from the complete novice to the expert. Other materials and unusual gift items are also available. The Guild also run courses from the site as well as producing a comprehensive book list.

## Falkiner Fine Papers

**Address**   76 Southampton Row
London
WC1
**Tel**   020 7831 1151
**Fax**   020 7430 1248
**Opening hours**
Mon-Sat 9.30am – 5.30pm
**Services**
Mail order, catalogues

Located not that far from the British Museum and founded in 1973 as a supplier of artists papers. It now also stocks a small range of books on bookbinding, conservation and calligraphy. Although it looks like a trade-style outlet they are willing to assist with enquiries on any of their papers or products.

## Felicity J Warnes

**Address**   36 Gordon Road
Enfield
Middlesex
EN2 0PZ
**Tel**   020 8367 1661
**Fax**   020 8372 1035
**Email**
felicity@fjwarns.u-net.com
**Opening hours**
By appointment only
**Services**
Mail order, catalogues

In operation since 1980, Felicity Warnes is now the largest specialist dealer in books and ephemera on costume, fashion, lace, embroidery, knitting and textiles. This is not a shop you can make an unarranged visit to so please telephone for an appointment to view the stock or to find out if they have that particular book you're looking for.

## RD Franks

**Address**   Kent House
Market Place
London
W1N 8EJ
**Tel**   020 7636 1244
**Fax**   020 7436 4904
**Email**
rdfranks@btinternet.com
**Opening hours**
Mon-Fri 9am – 5pm

Right in the heart of London's fashion district just behind Oxford Circus, R.D. Franks has been serving the fashion industry for over 100 years. For anyone with an interest in fashion, whether a student or professional designer, they stock the largest range of books and magazines on the topic available anywhere. Along with the books is workroom equipment, videos, CDs and computer-aided design systems. All displayed with the flair and imagination you would expect.

## Garden Books

**Address**   11 Blenheim Crescent
London
W11
**Tel**   020 7792 0777
**Opening hours**
Mon-Sat 9am – 6pm

Devoted entirely to gardening and complete with an in-store fountain, a display of garden tools and garden bench. A horticultural heaven, they cover all aspects of gardening from design to plant encyclopaedias, with plenty of new, out-of-print and secondhand books to suit the beginner and the expert. A visit here is easily combined with one to the Travel Bookshop and Books for Cooks – three of the best specialist bookshops in town.

## High Stakes

**Address**   21 Great Ormond Street
London
WC1N 3RA
**Tel**   020 7430 1021
**Fax**   020 7430 0021
**Web**
www.highstakes.co.uk
**Email**
info@highstakes.co.uk
**Opening hours**
Tues-Fri 11.30am – 5.30pm, Sat 11am – 5pm
**Services**
Mail order, catalogues

The only shop dedicated to the art and science of the noble wager. This tiny shop was opened in November 1998 by Ion Mills, a long-time gambler, greyhound owner and publisher (are they connected?). It looks more like an office than a shop and is somewhat off the beaten track but this won't deter hardened professionals from discovering myriad ways to lose the shirt off your back. Apart from books on every aspect of gambling they also keep CD-ROMs and have a No-Exit Press crime section

## Intercol London

**Address**   Camden Passage
114 High Street
Islington
London
N1 8DY
**Tel**   020 7354 2599
**Opening hours**
Wed-Sat 9.30am – 5.30pm

Located in the popular Camden Passage antiques market and a true specialist in playing cards, gambling, coins and notes, old maps and a few books on antiques.

## The Kew Shop

**Address**   Royal Botanic Gardens
Kew
London
TW9 3AB
**Tel**   020 832 5170
**Opening hours**
Mon-Sun 10am – 6pm

The world of gardening in every detail from 'how to' books, through garden design to scholarly books on botany from around the globe. Not surprisingly, given the subject specialisation, illustrated books are a particular strong point and there is also a range of general natural history titles, especially on birds. A nice touch is the selection of books for younger visitors.

## Lloyd's of Kew

**Address**   9 Mortlake Terrace
Kew
London
TW9 3DT
**Tel**   020 8940 2512
**Opening hours**
Tues-Sat 10.30am – 5.30pm, Sun 2pm – 5pm

Located off Kew Green and within only a few minutes' walk of Kew

Gardens, this specialist bookshop covers new and secondhand books on every aspect of botany and gardening. They also have a sub-specialisation in books on Italy – travel and history – in Italian and English.

## LCP Bookshop

**Address**    London College of Printing
Elephant and Castle
London
SE1 6SB
**Tel**    020 7514 6500 (ask for shop)
**Opening hours**
Term time only

Small college shop located at the London College of Printing. Stocks are small but it's a specialised range of books on printing and graphic design as well as a standard range of student stationery.

## Museum of Garden History

**Address**    Lambeth Palace Road
London
SE1 7LB
**Tel**    020 7261 1891
**Fax**    020 7401 8869
**Opening hours**
Mon-Fri 10.30am – 4pm, Sun 10.30am – 5pm (closed Sat)

This specialist museum concentrates on garden history from the 17th century onwards and is open from the first Sunday in March to the second Sunday in December. The gift shop stocks an impressive range of both general and reference books covering all topics from garden

design to how to care for specific plants. Other merchandise includes gardening implements, gifts and seeds.

## Shepherds, Sangorski and Sutcliffe

**Address**    76 Rochester Row
London
SW1P 1JU
**Tel**    020 7620 0060
**Fax**    020 7928 1813
**Opening hours**
Mon-Fri 9am – 5.30pm, Sat 10.30am – 5pm
**Email**
shepherds@bookbinding.co.uk

Sangorski and Sutcliffe Zaehnsdorf became 'Shepherds' after over 150 years in business as craft book-binders. Experts in bookbinding, restoration and paper conservation, they also stock binding materials, a superb range of quality papers, blank books and address books.

## Spink and Son

**Address**    5-7 King Street
St James's
London
SW1Y 6QS
**Tel**    020 7930 7888
**Fax**    020 7839 4853
**Opening hours**
Mon-Fri 9.30am – 5.30pm

Established as long ago as 1666, this world-renowned dealer main-tains the largest stock anywhere of out-of-print, new and rare books on numismatics. The book section is located on an upper floor. It is not as intimidating as it might first appear and all visitors and collectors are made welcome.

## Stanley Gibbons

**Address**   399 Strand
London
WC2R 0LX
**Tel**   020 7836 8444
**Opening hours**
Mon-Fri 8.30am – 6pm, Sat 9.30am – 5.30pm

**Services**
Catalogue, mail order

World famous as a premier stamp collector and dealer, this shop has occupied this portion of the Strand for over 100 years. Specialist titles and out-of-print literature on anything and everything to do with stamp collecting and postal systems make this a destination shop for philatelists from all over the world.

# Notes

# Environment & Nature

**Alternative Technology • Animals • Ecology • Gardening • Horses
Organic Farming • Ornithology • Reptiles • Waste Management**

## Crosskeys Select Books

**Address**  Colliers Row Road
Romford
Essex
RM5 2BH
**Tel**  020 8590 3604
**Fax**  020 8599 6177
**Web**
www.crosskeysbook.com
**Email**
crosskeys@dial.pipex.com
**Opening hours**
Mon-Fri 9am – 5pm, Sat 9am – 4pm
**Services**
Events, mail order, catalogues

A truly unique bookshop devoted to books on cats, dogs, horses and birds and by their own admission they have 'the biggest selection of books and videos in this field' in the world. Possibly one of few such specialists in the whole country, they have a website and operate a mail order service for customers further afield.

## Garden Books

**Address**  11 Blenheim Crescent
London
W11
**Tel**  020 7792 0777

*See Crafts & Pastimes*

## In Focus

**Address**  8-10 Royal Opera Arcade
Pall Mall
London

SW1

**Tel**     020 7839 1881
**Opening hours**
Mon-Fri 10.30am – 5.45pm, Sat 10am
– 4pm

Primarily a specialist in optical
equipment – binoculars and tele-
scopes – they have a comprehensive
collection of field guides and bird
identification books.

## Intermediate Technology

**Address**   103-105 Southampton Row
        London
        WC1B 4HH
**Tel**     020 7436 9761
**Fax**     020 7436 2013
**Web**
www.oneworld.org/itdg/publishers.html
**Email**
orders@itpubs.org.uk
**Opening hours**
Mon-Fri 9.30am – 6pm, Sat 11am –
6pm
**Services**
Mail order, catalogues

Dedicated to the furtherance of self-
reliance in developing countries, the
IT Bookshop specialises in books to
enable people to develop and use
productive technologies and
methods to gain greater control
over their lives. Their own publications of handbooks, manuals and
case studies adds to the authoritative range of stock on agriculture,
building, energy, enterprise development, health and water conservation. In addition there are books on
wider aid issues for academics and
professionals in the field.

## JG Natural History Books

**Address**   17 Streatham Vale
        Streatham
        London
        SW16 5SE
**Tel/Fax**   020 8764 4669
**Opening hours**
Mon-Fri 10am – 6pm (closed Wed), Sat
10am – 5pm
**Services**
Mail order, catalogues

Opposite Streatham Common railway station is this fascinating bookshop selling new and secondhand
books on reptiles, amphibians and
gemmology. The catalogue lists an
extensive number of books on these
topics. Having purchased a book on
how to keep a pet snake you can
pop into the pet shop next door to
buy the real thing.

## Kew Gardens Bookshop

**Address**   Royal Botanical Gardens
        Kew
        TW9 3AB
**Tel**     020 8332 5170

*See Crafts & Pastimes*

## Natural History Museum Bookshop

**Address**   Natural History Museum
        Cromwell Road
        London
        SW7 5BD
**Tel**     020 7938 9022
**Fax**     020 7938 8880

**Opening hours**
Mon-Sat 10am – 5.45pm, Sun 11am – 5.45pm

As you would expect this popular museum has a bookshop with an impressive range of books on natural history along with an array of cards, gifts and other products. The shop is located in gallery 37. The earth gallery has a shop of its own in gallery 60.

## Maya Books

**Address**   PO Box 379
            Twickenham
            TW1 2SU
**Tel**       020 8287 7964
**Fax**       020 8287 9068
**Web**
www.mayabooks.ndirect.co.uk
**Email**
sales@mayabooks.ndirect.co.uk

**Services**
Mail order, internet ordering

Although not a bookshop, this mail order and internet bookseller covers a range of subjects not widely available in one place. Covering areas from waste management to organic farming and ecological building, they offer a wide range of literature to help you on the way to a more environmentally friendly lifestyle. Their mission is to 'empower the little man, showing people they do have a choice and bring back the sense of community'. With links to websites dealing with similar subjects and a searchable brochure on floppy disk, all you need is access to a computer and you can begin to make the world a better place.

# Notes

# *General*

## E & R Abbott

**Address**   132-134 George Lane
South Woodford
London
E18 1BA
**Tel**   020 8989 6164
**Fax**   020 8989 1830
**Opening hours**
Mon-Fri 9am – 5.30pm, Sat 9am – 5pm

Mainly a stationery retailer
although they do have a general
range of popular paperbacks.

## Addison's

**Address**   137-139 Balham High Road
London
SW12 9AV
**Tel**   020 8675 1143
**Opening hours**
Mon-Sat 8.30am – 6pm

A good local bookshop with bestsellers and a general stock. There is
a leaning towards children's books.

## Angel Bookshop

**Address**   102 Islington High Street
London
N1 8EG
**Tel**   020 7226 2904
**Opening hours**
Mon-Sun 9.30am – 6pm

Catering to their antique dealer
neighbours in Islington's Camden
Passage, this small general bookshop has a reasonable antiques and
collecting section. The shop has a
literary bent and the work of local
authors is prominently displayed
and well represented.

## Baines Bookshop

| | |
|---|---|
| **Address** | 3 Lower Square |
| | Civic Centre |
| | Sutton |
| | Surrey |
| | SM1 1EA |
| **Tel** | 020 8661 1677 |

**Opening hours**
Mon-Fri 9am – 5.30pm (Wed 9am – 1pm), Sat 9am – 5pm
**Services**
Mail order

Situated in the Sutton civic centre which also houses the local library and adult education establishment. The subject range is what you would expect from a well-stocked local bookshop and caters for most tastes along with an obvious range of academic and language books for the local students.

## Banana Bookshop

| | |
|---|---|
| **Address** | 10 The Market |
| | The Piazza |
| | Covent Garden |
| | London |
| | WC2E |
| **Tel** | 020 7379 7475 |

**Opening hours**
Mon-Sat 10am – 8pm, Sun 11am – 6pm

It looks deceptively small from the outside and on busy days it's hard to get in let alone find room to browse. However, venture in and discover a basement packed with all manner of books at discounted prices. The range covers children's, travel, sport, cookery and fiction. Maybe the name is a reference to what the market once sold.

## Bargain Book Centre

| | |
|---|---|
| **Address** | Orchards Shopping Centre |
| | Dartford |
| | Kent |
| | DA1 IDN |
| **Tel** | 01322 284075 |

**Opening hours**
Mon- Sat 9am – 5.30pm

A general remainder bookshop with decent books at low prices.

## Bargain Bookshop

| | |
|---|---|
| **Address** | 2 The Concourse |
| | Edmonton |
| | London |
| | N9 0TY |
| **Tel** | 020 8807 7972 |

**Opening hours**
Mon 9.30am – 4.30pm, Tues Sat 9.30am – 5.30pm

A substantial collection of bargain books at reasonable prices provides the main the interest at this shop.

## Barnards Bookshop

| | |
|---|---|
| **Address** | 50 Windsor Street |
| | Uxbridge |
| | Middlesex |
| | UB8 1AB |
| **Tel** | 01895 232751 |
| **Fax** | 01895 270164 |

**Opening hours**
Mon-Sat 9am – 5.30pm
**Services**
Mail order

Barnards have been involved in bookselling since 1944 and at the present Uxbridge location since 1975. This good old-fashioned general bookshop deals with all the popular subject areas.

## Beaumonts Books

**Address**   60 Church Road
             Barnes
             London
             SW13 0DQ
**Tel**       020 8741 0786
**Opening hours**
Mon-Sat 9.30am – 5.30pm

A local bookshop in the best sense of the word. Host to a good general range of books with helpful, friendly staff demonstrated by the free local delivery service they offer.

## Beckenham Bookshop

**Address**   42 High Street
             Beckenham
             Kent
             BR3 1AY
**Tel**       020 8650 9744
**Fax**       020 8402 7886
**Web**
www.beckenhambooks.co.uk
**Email**
books@orma.co.uk
**Opening hours**
Mon-Sat 9.30am – 5.30pm
**Services**
Mail order, catalogues, events, signings

Serving the local area for 15 years with a good range of fiction, local history and children's titles.

## Beckett's Bookshop

**Address**   6 Bellevue Road
             Wandsworth Common
             London
             SW17 7EG
**Tel**       020 8672 4413
**Fax**       020 8672 1561
**Email**
beckbooks@aol.com
**Opening hours**
Mon-Sat 9.30am – 6pm
**Services**
Mail order, catalogues

As far as we know, the only bookshop in London where in winter you are greeted by a tempting selection of new books and an open fire. On summer days Wandsworth Common opposite is a good place to sit and read.

## Bestsellers

**Address**   46 High Road
             East Finchley
             London
             N2 9PJ
**Tel**       020 8883 5354
**Fax**       020 8883 7686
**Opening hours**
Mon-Sat 8am – 6.30pm (Thurs 8am – 8pm)

Current bestsellers, hardback and paperback, all at discounted prices.

## Bibliophile

**Address**   5 Thomas Road
             London, E14 7BN
**Tel**       020 7575 9222
**Fax**       020 7538 4115
**Email**
bibliophilebooks@btinternet.com
**Opening hours**
Mon-Fri 8.30am – 5pm
**Services**
Mail order, catalogues

Primarily a mail order company. However it does have a large warehouse in Docklands and boasts some of the lowest prices around for bargain and remainder books.

## Bolingbroke Bookshop

**Address**    147 Northcote Road
Battersea
London
SW11 6QB
**Tel**    020 7223 9344
**Opening hours**
Mon-Sat 9.30am – 6pm, Sun 11am –
4pm

Owned by Pipeline Bookshops and supplied by their quick and comprehensive wholesale business. It retains a strong community feel, covering most subjects with a particular strength in children's books.

## Book House

**Branch**    24 Torrington Place
London
WC1E
**Tel**    020 7631 4383
**Opening hours**
Mon-Sat 10am – 6.30pm, Sun noon – 6pm

**Branch**    Unit 14
Villiers Street
London
WC2N
**Tel**    020 7839 8424
**Opening hours**
Mon-Sat 9am – 9pm, Sun 11am – 9pm

**Branch**    14 Church Street
Greenwich
London
SE10 9BJ
**Tel**    020 8305 1975
**Opening hours**
Mon-Fri 10am – 6pm (Tues closed),
Sat, Sun 10.30am – 6.30pm

**Branch**    21-22 Upper Street
Islington
London
N1
**Tel**    020 7354 2637
**Opening hours**
Mon-Sat 9.30am – 6.30pm, Sun 11am – 5pm

The Book House shops carry a standard selection of remainders and bargain books with a few cards, calendars and other stationery items thrown in.

## Books etc

**Address**    120 Charing Cross Road
London
WC2H 0JR
**Tel**    020 7379 6838
**Opening hours**
Mon-Sat 9.30am – 8pm, Sun noon – 6pm

Once the flagship store of the Books etc chain, and although now overshadowed by its bigger brother Borders on Oxford Street (this branch will soon be renamed Borders), it is still one of the best general bookshops in London, especially for new books.

## Book Warehouse

**Address**    120 Southampton Row
London
WCIB 5AA
**Tel**    020 7242 1119
**Fax**    020 7404 5636
**Opening hours**
Mon-Fri 8.30am – 10pm, Sat 9am – 10pm, Sun 10am – 10pm

Cheap books at low prices.

## Bookseller Crow on the Hill

**Address**   50 Weston Street
Crystal Palace
London
SE19 3AF
**Tel**   020 8771 8831
**Fax**   020 8771 8831
**Web**
www.bookseller.com
**Email**
booksellercrow@btinternet.com
**Opening hours**
Mon-Fri 9am – 7.30pm, Sat 9am –
6.30pm, Sun 11am – 5pm
**Services**
Mail order, catalogues, events, signings,
readings

An independent bookshop with
heaving shelves and an informal
atmosphere. Tired customers can
relax on chairs and there is a kids'
play area. All subjects are covered
well with particular strength in
contemporary fiction and children's.
Apart from books they carry a
number of literary magazines
including the *Literary Review* and
the *London Review of Books*.

## The Bookshop

**Address**   150 High Road
Loughton
IG10 4BE
**Tel**   020 8508 9855
**Fax**   020 8508 9855
**Opening hours**
Mon-Sat 9am – 5.30pm

Serving Loughton for over 30 years
with a variety of popular subjects
and bestsellers in hardback and
paperback.

## The Bookshop

**Address**   51 High Street
Ruislip
Middlesex
HA4 7BD
**Tel**   01895 678269
**Web**
www.bookshop.co.uk
**Email**
bookhc@bic.unet.co.uk
**Opening hours**
Mon-Sat 9am – 5.30pm
**Services**
Mail order

Centrally located on the High
Street, a modest bookshop offering
books, cards, videos and giftwrap
to local shoppers.

## Bookshop Islington Green

**Address**   76 Upper Street
Islington Green
London
N1 0NU
**Tel**   020 7359 4699
**Fax**   020 7354 9855
**Opening hours**
Mon-Sat 10am – 10pm, Sun noon –
6pm
**Services**
Mail order

The late opening hours and its
proximity to the Screen on the
Green cinema next door contribute
to a great-for-browsing independent
bookshop. The choice of recently
published books is particularly
appealing and they seem to be well
in tune with their local customer
base.

## Bookstop

**Address**  375 Upper Richmond Road
West
East Sheen
London
SW17 7NX
**Tel/Fax**  020 8876 1717
**Opening hours**
Mon-Sat 9.30am – 6pm

A selection of new books on the main subject areas is the order of the day in this particular bookshop.

## Bookstore

**Address**  44 High Street
Walton-On-Thames
Surrey
KT12 1BY
**Tel**  01932 254455
**Fax**  01932 254716
**Opening hours**
Mon-Fri 9am – 6pm, Sat 9am –
5.30pm

A general range of books with most popular bases covered constitutes a good local bookshop for the Walton area.

## Bookworld

**Branch**  12 Ealing Broadway Centre
Ealing
London
W5 2NU
**Tel**  020 8840 7355
**Fax**  0208 840 5769
**Opening hours**
Mon-Fri 9am – 8.30pm, Sat 9am –
7.30pm, Sun 10am – 5.30pm

**Branch**  121-123 North End
Croydon
Surrey

CR0 1TL
**Tel**  020 8681 0159
**Fax**  020 8667 0835
**Opening hours**
Mon-Fri 8.30am – 6.30pm (Thurs
8.30am – 9pm), Sat 8.30am – 7pm, Sun
9.30am – 5.30pm

**Branch**  40a Clarence Street
Kingston upon Thames
Surrey
KT1 1NR
**Tel**  020 8549 2110
**Fax**  020 8549 1637
**Opening hours**
Mon-Thurs 8.30am – 7pm, Fri 8.30am
– 7.15pm, Sat 8.30am – 7pm, Sun
10am – 6pm

General stock featuring bestsellers, popular new books at discounted prices and a few bargain books.

## Borders

**Address**  197-213 Oxford Street
London
W1R 1AH
**Tel**  020 7292 1600
**Fax**  020 7292 1616
**Opening hours**
Mon-Sat 8am – 11pm, Sun noon – 6pm

Long hours and have-a-nice-day ambience make this American-style bookstore, occupying what was once a department store, a great bookshop on Oxford Street. Although the stock range is huge, the thoughtful design and clear signage makes it easy to browse. The magazine department alone is worth a visit and captures something of the flavour of a New York newsstand with a tempting selection of periodicals from both sides of the

Atlantic. Escalators transport customers through the centre of the shop and you'll always find browsers flicking through prospective purchases whilst enjoying a coffee in the shop. It's the shape of things to come in Britain's largest cities and is clearly a hit with the capital's book-buyers and visitors alike, even though waiting in line at the ground-floor checkouts can be a frustrating end to a great shopping experience.

## Bush Books

| | |
|---|---|
| **Address** | 113 Shepherds Bush Centre |
| | Shepherds Bush |
| | London |
| | W12 8PP |
| **Tel** | 020 8749 7652 |
| **Fax** | 020 8749 7652 |

**Opening hours**
Mon-Sat 10am – 6pm

Fiction, travel and media studies (BBC centre is nearby) are well covered in this general bookshop.

## Camden Lock Books and Prints

| | |
|---|---|
| **Address** | 77 Camden Lock Place |
| | London |
| | NW1 8AF |
| **Tel** | 020 7267 3824 |

**Web**
www.camdenlockbooks.com/uk
**Opening hours**
Mon-Fri 11.30am – 4.30pm, Sat, Sun 10.30am – 5.30pm

At the heart of the popular and very busy Camden Lock market, the main attraction is new paperbacks at up to a price-busting 50% off. Subject areas covered include fiction, crime, science fiction, media, psychology and health plus a few secondhand books.

## Cannings

| | |
|---|---|
| **Address** | 181 High Street |
| | New Malden |
| | Surrey |
| | KT3 4BL |
| **Tel** | 020 8942 0450 |

**Opening hours**
Mon-Sat 9am – 5.30pm

A family-run shop since 1935 housed in a converted Victorian house. Apart from selling books they also stock toys, stationery, greeting cards and, intriguingly, Belgian chocolates.

## Chener Books

| | |
|---|---|
| **Address** | 14 Lordship Lane |
| | London |
| | SE22 8HN |
| **Tel** | 020 8299 0771 |
| **Fax** | 020 8299 0771 |

**Opening hours**
Mon-Sat 10am – 6pm

The stock here covers all the general subjects particularly biography, drama, literature, science fiction and history.

## Chorleywood Bookshop

| | |
|---|---|
| **Address** | 4 New Parade |
| | Whiteland Avenue |
| | Chorleywood |
| | Herts |
| | WD3 5NJ |

**Tel** 01923 283566
**Fax** 01923 283566
**Email**
cwbookshop@aol.com
**Opening hours**
Mon-Sat 9am – 5.30pm

Centrally located in Chorleywood village, this bookshop was established 25 years ago by a local author who sold out to two of his regular customers in 1998. It is a good-value local bookshop with a particular strength in children's books.

## Compendium Books

**Address** 234 High Street
Camden
London
NW1 8QS
**Tel** 020 7485 8944
020 7267 1525
**Fax** 020 7267 0193
**Web**
www.compendiumbooks.com
**Email**
compbks@dircom.co.uk
**Opening hours**
Mon-Wed 10am – 6pm, Thurs-Sat 10am – 7pm, Sun noon – 6pm

*See Politics & Social Sciences*

## Corbett's Bookshop

**Address** 19-21 High Street
Pinner
Middlesex
HA5 5PJ
**Tel** 020 8866 4022
**Fax** 020 8866 3956
**Opening hours**
Mon-Fri 9am – 5.30pm

A well established general book-

shop with a substantial stock range and a loyal customer base.

## Crime In Store

**Address** 14 Bedford Street
Covent Garden
London
WC2 9HE
**Tel** 020 7379 3795
**Fax** 020 7379 8988
**Opening hours**
Mon-Sat 10.30am – 6.30pm, Sun (June-Sept) noon – 5pm

This innovative shop is part-owned by leading crime writers Colin Dexter and Minette Walters and was opened in 1996 to fill the need for a dedicated mystery and thriller bookshop in central London. It is a worthy showcase for the chosen genre and the range includes signed first editions, audio books and secondhand stock. Events are held almost weekly and a specialist catalogue is produced six times a year. More than a bookshop, being a customer is like joining a club.

## Dillons

**Address** 82 Gower Street
London
WC1E 6EQ
**Tel** 020 7636 1577/7467 1698
**Fax** 020 7580 7680
**Web**
www.dillons.co.uk
**Opening hours**
Mon-Fri 9am – 7pm, Sat 9.30am – 6pm, Sun 11am – 5pm

With the growth of book superstores 30,000 square feet doesn't sound very impressive, but Dillons Gower Street is still one of the best-stocked and best-known bookshops in London with a well-deserved reputation that stretches back to its foundation by Una Dillon. Nevertheless, this heritage looks likely to be traded in for a new name – Waterstone's – although the academic prowess will undoubtedly remain.

## Dulwich Books

**Address**    6 Croxted Road
West Dulwich
London
SE21 8SW
**Tel/Fax**    020 8670 1920
*See Children's*

## Dulwich Village Bookshop

**Address**    1d Calton Road
Dulwich Village
London
SE21 7DE
**Tel**    020 8693 2808
**Fax**    020 8693 2752
**Opening hours**
Mon-Sat 9am – 5.30pm
**Services**
Events, signings, mail order

There has been a bookshop on this site for approaching 50 years. Once called the Gallery Bookshop, the current shop was acquired by two ex-Waterstone's directors in 1996. The result is a model local book-shop with a good range of new titles and backlist, an efficient special order service and a discount scheme for book groups.

## Eastcote Bookshop

**Address**    156-158 Field End Road
Eastcote
Pinner
Middlesex
HA5 1RH
**Tel**    020 8866 9888
**Fax**    020 8905 9387
**Opening hours**
Tues-Sat 10am – 5pm

A short walk from Eastcote tube station, this pleasant shop opened in 1995. It is a general bookshop whose claim to fame is providing good books and good service.

## Eastside Bookshop

**Address**    178 Whitechapel Road
London
E1 1BJ
**Tel**    020 7247 0216
**Fax**    020 7247 2882
**Opening hours**
Mon-Fri 10am – 5.30pm, Sat 10am – 5pm

Sandwiched between the post office and the London Hospital opposite Whitechapel tube. They have a general range of stock but are particularly strong on local history, including books on Jack the Ripper and the Kray Twins. They also host writers groups and offer bursary awards for local authors.

## Elaine's

**Address**   67 Darkes Lane
Potters Bar
Herts
EN6 1BJ
**Tel**   01707 654032
**Opening hours**
Mon-Sat 9am – 5.30pm

Handily located near the local railway station.

## Elgin Books

**Address**   6 Elgin Crescent
London
W11 2HX
**Tel**   020 7229 2186
**Fax**   020 7792 1457
**Opening hours**
Tues-Sat 10am – 6pm

This attractive general bookshop with a literary feel has a well-chosen selection of fiction, poetry, drama and children's books among other general subjects. Current book reviews are on display and the shop noticeboard acts as a local information exchange point.

## Eltham Books

**Address**   8 Chequers Parade
Eltham
London
SE9
**Tel**   020 8859 4479
**Opening hours**
Mon-Sat 9am – 5.30pm

Fiction and biography are the bread and butter of this local bookshop. Both new and secondhand books can be found and the shop also offers a buy-back service.

## Fielders

**Address**   54 Wimbledon Hill Road
Wimbledon
London
SW19 7PA
**Tel**   020 8946 5044
**Fax**   020 8944 1320
**Opening hours**
Mon-Sat 9am – 5.30pm

A stationery supplier on the ground floor but upstairs is a long-established general book department. The travel and map section is reasonable and includes a good stock of Ordnance Survey maps.

## Finchley Bookshop

**Address**   98 Ballards Lane
London
N3 2DN
**Tel**   020 8346 7761
**Email**
facultybooks@compuserve.com
**Opening hours**
Mon-Sat 9.30am – 5.30pm

A family concern for over 30 years, run first by Hilda and Norman Hart now taken on by their son Michael. As ever with this style of local general bookshop, children's books are a speciality.

## Foyles

**Address**   113-119 Charing Cross
Road
London, WC2H 0EB
**Tel**   020 7437 5660
**Opening hours**
Mon-Sat 9am – 6pm (Thurs 9am – 7pm)

Faced with the progressive might of Waterstone's, Dillons and Books etc over the years, it is a surprise to many how Foyles managed to survive as the book retailing revolution gathered pace in the '80s and '90s. Owning the freehold and leaving the shop as it was have contributed most to Foyles' longevity. Unbelievably archaic practices and a jumble of books represented a business opportunity to the sharp-suited go-getters who competed for the right to convert Foyles into a temple of modern book retailing – they failed miserably to persuade matriarch owner Christina Foyle to sell the family silver. Now she's gone, Foyles' foibles might yet become a unique selling proposition.

## Gay's the Word

**Address**   66 Marchmont Street
London
WC1N 1AB
**Tel**   020 7278 7654
**Email**
gays.theword@virgin.net
**Opening hours**
Mon-Sat 10am – 6.30pm, Sun 2pm – 6pm

A comprehensive range of books of gay and lesbian interest along with a good selection of general titles. Stationery, cards, magazines and newspapers complete the stock range.

## Gilbert's Bookshop

**Address**   26 Circus Road
London
NW8 6PD
**Tel**   020 7722 8863
**Fax**   020 7722 3540

**Opening hours**
Mon-Sat 8am – 6.30pm

Located in the heart of St John's Wood, this friendly shop has been supplying the local population with a modest range of new books for over 15 years. Most subjects are covered including fiction, biography and travel.

## Greens the Bookcellar

**Address**   17 Marylebone High Street
London
W1M 3PD
**Tel**   020 7935 7227
**Opening hours**
Mon-Fri 9am – 5.45pm, Sat 9am – 4pm, Sun 9am – noon

Found in the basement of Mr and Mrs Green's newsagents is Mr Green junior's 'bookcellar'. It's a popular local bookshop with a large and varied range of both new and backlist fiction, plus a few bargains.

## Greenwich Book Time

**Branch**   44 Greenwich Church Street
Greenwich
London
SE10 9BL
**Tel**   020 8293 3902
**Opening hours**
Mon-Thurs 10am – 6pm, Fri-Sun 10am – 9pm

**Branch**   37 King William Walk
Greenwich
London
SE10 9HD
**Tel**   020 8858 5789
**Opening hours**

Mon-Sun 10am – 6pm

**Branch** 277 Greenwich High Road
Greenwich
London
SE10 8NB
**Tel** 020 8293 0096
**Opening hours**
Mon-Sun 10am – 6pm (winter), Mon-Sun 10am – 10pm (summer)

Three shops make up this mini chain in Greenwich specialising in the cheapest of bargain books with many items for only £1.

## Hammond Roberts

**Address** 136-138 Field End Road
Eastcote
Pinner
Middlesex
HA5 1RH
**Tel** 020 8868 5786
**Fax** 020 8868 8491
**Email**
sat41@hotmail.com
**Opening hours**
Mon-Fri 9am – 5.30pm

Local independent bookshop with a good range of general books.

## Hatchards

**Address** 187 Piccadilly
London
W1V 0LE
**Tel** 020 7439 9921
**Fax** 020 7494 1313
**Email**
187picc@hatchards.co.uk
**Opening hours**
Mon-Sat 9am – 6pm, Sun noon – 6pm
**Services**
Mail order, events, readings, signings

This London landmark was founded in 1797 by John Hatchard and holds all four Royal Warrants. It has a literary and historic pedigree second to none (the Abolition of Slavery Bill was signed by William Wilberforce on the premises) and its customers include book-loving tourists from all over the world, the great and the good in this country and ex-pats overseas. There are five floors of books comprehensively covering all general subjects. Fiction, biography, gardening (The Royal Horticultural Society was founded in this building), crafts and natural history are superbly stocked and include the cream of backlist titles. The rare books, first editions and fine bindings department recreates the ambience of Hatchards past and a book search service operates to find lost treasures of the book world. In the autumn of 1999 Waterstone's will be opening Europe's largest bookstore in what was once Simpson's department store just along the road from Hatchards. Regardless of what or who else is located nearby (and the renaming of Dillons in Gower Street), it's easy to conclude that Hatchards will continue to thrive on name and reputation alone, for the forseeable future at least.

## Henry Stokes & Co.

**Address** 58 Elizabeth Street
London
SW1W 9PB

**Tel** 020 7730 7073
**Fax** 020 7730 5568
**Opening hours**
Mon-Fri 9.30am – 6pm, Sat 9.30am – 1pm

Founded in 1861 as a stationers and bookshop and situated on the corner of Elizabeth Street and Chester Row in the heart of Belgravia. Current fiction, non-fiction, biography, cookery, gardening and interiors are the main areas. They also continue to provide a printing service on the stationery side.

## Heywood Hill

**Address** 10 Curzon Street
London
W1Y 7FJ
**Tel** 020 7629 0647

*See Literature*

## Highgate Bookshop

**Address** 9 Highgate High Street
London
N6 5JR
**Tel** 020 8348 8202
**Fax** 020 8348 5989
**Opening hours**
Mon-Sat 10am – 6pm, Sun noon – 5pm
**Services**
Mail order

Twenty years a local bookshop and although on the small side they offer a well-selected range of new titles in keeping with their local customer base. A particular feature is the support given to local books and local authors, with many signed copies available inside.

## Holloway Stationers and Booksellers

**Address** 357 Holloway Road
London
N7 0RN
**Tel** 020 7607 3972
**Fax** 020 7607 3972
**Opening hours**
Mon-Sat 9am – 6pm

Books, primarily paperbacks, compete with a large range of stationery for space. All the popular subject areas are here, from new age to social studies.

## Houbens Bookshop

**Address** 2 Church Court
Richmond
Surrey
TW9 1JL
**Tel** 020 8940 1055
**Fax** 020 8332 9788
**Email**
houbens@dial.pipex.com
**Opening hours**
Mon-Sat 10am – 6pm

Located in a pedestrian alley in central Richmond, they offer a good mix of new and secondhand books specialising particularly in the arts, social sciences and humanities. The academic side is strengthened by a comprehensive range of textbooks.

## IBIS Bookshop

**Address** 109 High Street
Burgh Heath
Banstead
Surrey
SM7 2NJ
**Tel** 01737 353260

**Fax**    01737 371205
**Opening hours**
Tues-Sat 9am – 5.30pm

Originally established in 1938, IBIS have long enjoyed a reputation for good books and first-class service to the residents of Banstead and the surrounding area. New books are a particular strength in this small shop.

# John Lewis

**Branch**    Book Department
        Wood Street
        Kingston upon Thames
        Surrey
        KT1 1TE
**Tel**    020 8547 3000
**Fax**    020 8547 4210
**Opening hours**
Tues, Wed 9.30am – 6pm, Thurs, Fri 9.30am – 8pm, Sat 9am – 6pm

**Branch**    Book Department
        Oxford Street
        London
        W1A 1EX
**Tel**    020 7629 7711
**Fax**    020 7629 7712
**Opening hours**
Mon-Fri 9.30am – 6pm (Thurs 10am – 8pm), Sat 9am – 6pm

*See Children's*

# Joseph's Bookstore

**Address**    1255/1257 Finchley Road
        London
        NW11 0AD
**Tel**    020 8731 7575
**Fax**    020 8731 6699
**Opening hours**
Mon-Fri 9.30am – 6.30pm, Sat-Sun

10am – 5pm
**Services**
Mail order, readings, signings

A thriving independent bookshop in the heart of the local community. Aside from the usual range they also have a large stock of remainder books and a strong Jewish section. They play host to regular author events and with a café planned to open in the future this is a popular place for browsing.

# Junction Books

**Address**    Unit 6
        The Junction
        St Johns Hill
        London
        SW11 1RU
**Tel**    020 7738 9551
**Opening hours**
Mon-Fri 8.30am – 8.30pm, Sat 9.30am – 8.30pm, Sun noon – 6pm

A selection of new books in the popular subject areas – particularly paperbacks – are to found here in the shopping centre adjoining Clapham Junction station.

# Kew Bookshop

**Address**    1 Station Approach
        Richmond
        Surrey
        TW9 3QB
**Tel/Fax**    020 8940 0030
**Opening hours**
Mon-Sat 10am – 6pm
**Services**
Events, signings

A small but prominent bookshop in the heart of Kew Village at the entrance to the underground station. They offer a good varied selection on most general subjects with a particularly strong children's section. They also like to feature the work of local authors.

## Kirkdale Bookshop

**Address**    272 Kirkdale
          Sydenham
          London
          SE26 4RS
**Tel**      020 8778 4701
**Opening hours**
Mon-Sat 9am – 5.30pm

A short walk from Sydenham railway station, this bookshop has been in business since England last won the football World Cup. It is a charming shop offering a wide choice of new and secondhand books rather than focusing on a particular topic.

## Langton's Bookshop

**Address**    44-45 Church Street
          Twickenham
          Middlesex
          TW1 3NT
**Tel**      020 8892 3800
**Fax**      020 8607 9726
**Email**
langtons.books@virgin.net
**Opening hours**
Mon-Sat 9.30am – 5.30pm

A reasonable range of paperbacks and hardbacks on offer at this local bookshop. They also have a selection of greetings cards.

## Liberty Book Dept

**Address**    210 Regent Street
          London
          W1R 6AH
**Tel**      020 7734 1234
**Fax**      020 7573 9876
**Opening hours**
Mon-Wed 9.30am – 6.30pm, Thurs 9.30am – 8pm, Fri 9.30am – 7pm, Sat 9.30am – 6.30pm
**Services**
Mail order

In this world-famous store is a book department to match the splendour and reputation of the Liberty name. The emphasis is on crafts, design, art, interiors, cookery and gardening.

## Murder One

**Address**    71-73 Charing Cross Road
          London
          WC2H 0AA
**Tel**      020 7734 3483
**Web**
www.murderone.co.uk
**Email**
murderonelondon@compuserve.com
**Opening hours**
Mon-Wed 10am – 7pm, Thurs-Sat 10am – 8pm
**Services**
Mail order, signings, events

A shop of three parts: fantasy, romance and crime. There is an extensive range of new and secondhand books on all three subjects, a great selection of American crime novels and they also sell mystery dinner party games. Furtive glancers with turned-up collars, Trekkies and not-so-new romantics all pay homage here.

## Muswell Hill Bookshop

**Address**   72 Fortis Green Road
Muswell Hill
London
N10 3HN
**Tel**   020 8444 7588
**Fax**   020 8442 0693
**Opening hours**
Mon-Sat 9.30am – 6pm, Sun noon – 5pm

Opposite the Muswell Hill Children's Bookshop is where residents of north London have to travel for this superb example of a local general bookshop. Literary events and author signings are a real feature and keep the locals coming back for more.

## Nomad Books

**Address**   781 Fulham Road
London
SW6 5HA
**Tel**   020 7736 4000
**Fax**   020 7736 9454

*See Travel*

## Notting Hill Books

**Address**   132 Palace Gardens Terrace
London
W8 4RT
**Tel**   020 7727 5988
**Opening hours**
Mon-Sat 10.15am – 6pm (Thurs 10.15am – 1pm)

Cheap secondhand paperbacks spill onto the pavement but inside the stock inclines towards art, literature, history and academic subjects. Paperbacks, remainders and secondhand books dominate with a smattering of recently published review copies. Good for browsing.

## Pan Bookshop

**Address**   158-162 Fulham Road
London
SW10 9PG
**Tel**   020 7373 4997
**Fax**   020 7370 0746
**Opening hours**
Mon-Fri 9.30am – 9.30pm, Sat 10am – 10pm, Sun 11am – 9pm

A well-established award-winning general bookshop, thoroughly deserving all the accolades received over the years. It covers all the major interest areas with panache and is a cut above most other general bookshops of comparable size. Signed copies are a feature as is a comprehensive and imaginative range of new titles.

## Pitshanger Bookshop

**Address**   141 Pitshanger Lane
Ealing
London
W5 1RH
**Tel/Fax**   020 8991 8131
**Opening hours**
Mon-Fri 9.30am – 6pm, Sat 9am – 6pm

Opened in 1995, this suburban bookshop is conveniently positioned next to the local library and has an adequate range of general books, cards, music and stationery.

## Primrose Hill Books

**Address**   134 Regent's Park Road
London
NW1 8XL
**Tel**   020 7586 2022
**Fax**   020 7722 9653
**Web**
www.primrosehillbooks.co.uk
**Email**
primrose@netcomuk.co.uk
**Opening hours**
Mon-Fri 9am – 6.30pm, Sat 10am –
6.30pm, Sun 11am – 6pm
**Services**
Mail order, events, catalogues, readings

The splendour of Regent's Park is within walking distance of this attractive late-Victorian building virtually on the doorstep of Primrose Hill Park. The two-storey shop is overflowing with good books – new and secondhand – and is perfect for finding the new biography or literary work you've just read a review on. The main subjects are fiction, biography, art, travel, history and children's but it's the new books that catch the eye. Another treasure among London's independent general bookshops.

## Prospero's Books

**Address**   32 Broadway
Crouch End
London
N8 9SU
**Tel**   020 8348 8900
**Fax**   020 8248 3604
**Email**
brichapel@aol.com
**Opening hours**
Mon-Sat 9.30am – 6.30pm, Sun

11.30am – 5.30pm

Located in the centre of trendy Crouch End and a hive of activity, particularly at the weekend. It's a small shop and this clearly restricts the number of books they can cram into the space available. The special order service makes up for what they don't have in stock.

## Regent Bookshop

**Address**   73 Parkway
London
NW1 7PP
**Tel**   020 7485 9822
**Fax**   020 7485 9822
**Email**
Jack@regentbookshop.freeserve
**Opening hours**
Mon-Sat 9am – 6.15pm, Sun noon –
6.30pm

Rather scruffy general shop on the edge of Camden.

## Riverside Bookshop

**Branch**   18-19 Hay's Galeria
Tooley Street
London
SE1 2HD
**Tel**   020 7378 1824
**Fax**   020 7407 5315
**Email**
Riverbkshp@aol.com
**Opening hours**
Mon-Fri 9.30am – 6pm

**Branch**   49 Shad Thames
Butlers Wharf
London
SE1 2NJ
**Tel**   020 7403 7750
**Fax**   020 8314 5966
**Opening hours**

Mon-Fri 9.30am – 6pm, Sat 10am – 6.30pm, Sun 11am – 6.30pm

Riverside have two branches both situated, no surprise here, by the river! The first is located in Hay's Galleria and the second in Shad Thames, an area undergoing major regeneration and the site of the planned London Assembly. Both branches are a delight to visit and offer the best features of bookshops determined to establish a loyal local following through good books and crisp service.

## Selfridges

| | |
|---|---|
| **Address** | 400 Oxford Street London W1A 1AB |
| **Tel** | 020 7629 1234 |
| **Fax** | 020 7495 8321 |

**Opening hours**
Mon-Wed 10am – 7pm, Thurs-Fri 10am – 8pm, Sat 9.30am – 7pm, Sun noon – 6pm

A better than average book department located in the basement of this famous department store. The department is well stocked and conducive to browsing. Seating is provided to rest weary legs.

## Soho Original Bookshop

| | |
|---|---|
| **Address** | 12 Brewer Street London W1R |
| **Tel** | 020 7494 1615 |
| **Fax** | 020 7439 2041 |

**Opening hours**
Mon-Sat 10am – 12.30am, Sun 11am – 11pm

Located in the heart of Soho and could be mistaken for the type of 'bookshop' once synonymous with the seedier characteristics of this part of London. They actually sell a good range of remainder and bargain books covering most subjects, with a particular strength in art, photography and cinema. If you do wish to purchase something a little stronger they keep more adult-orientated books below ground level.

## Stoke Newington Bookshop

| | |
|---|---|
| **Address** | 159 Stoke Newington High Street London N16 0NY |
| **Tel** | 020 7249 2808 |
| **Fax** | 020 7249 7845 |
| **Email** | |

snbooks@dialpipex.com
**Opening hours**
Mon-Sat 9.30am – 5.30pm, Sun 11am – 5pm

A bookshop that encourages browsing and buying with a varied range of quality books. It has a good reputation as a general bookshop built up by serving the local community over the last five years. Its strength lies in fiction and children's titles.

## Swan Library Booksellers

| | |
|---|---|
| **Address** | 27 Corbets Tey Road Upminster Essex |

RM14 2AR
**Tel** 01708 222930
**Fax** 01708 640378
**Opening hours**
Mon-Thurs, Sat 9am – 5.30pm, Fri
9am – 6pm
**Services**
Mail order, catalogues

A short stroll from Upminster
station leads you to this pleasant
little bookshop. It began in 1937 as
a lending library and library
supplier but is now solely a general
bookseller.

## Tac-Tic-Al Bookshop & Café

**Address** 26-27 D'Arblay Street
London
W1V 3SJ
**Tel** 020 7287 2823
**Opening hours**
Mon-Fri 10am – 11pm, Sat noon –
11pm, Sun noon – 10.30pm

Subjects in keeping with the distinct
character of the area are on offer in
this hip combined bar and bookshop. Popular culture, film, cinema
and the media make up the bulk of
an eclectic mix of books and
magazines.

## Talking Bookshop

**Address** 11 Wigmore Street
London
W1H 9LB
**Tel** 020 7491 4117
**Fax** 020 7629 1966
**Web**
www.talkingbooks.co.uk
**Email**
talkingbooks@msn.com

**Opening hours**
Mon-Sat 9.30am – 5.30pm
**Services**
Mail order, catalogues

Although located on Wigmore Street
the shop is a little off the well-worn
tracks around Oxford Street but it's
no handicap because if it's audio
books you're looking for then this is
the only place to visit. The range is
totally comprehensive and in the
unlikely event of the item you want
being out of stock, efficient staff will
happily order it in for you.

## Vermillion Books

**Address** 10a Acton Street
London
WC1R 4PD
**Tel** 020 7741 8375
**Opening hours**
Mon only noon – 6pm (other times by
appointment)

Previously located in Red Lion
Street and now to be found off
Gray's Inn Road. Despite the
restricted opening hours Vermillion
is well worth a visit for the varied
range of mainly recently published
hardbacks and paperbacks –
primarily review copies – at
discounts of up to 50%.

## Village Bookshop

**Address** 475 High Road
Woodford Green
Essex
IG8 0XE
**Tel** 020 8506 0551
**Fax** 020 8559 0156
**Email**

vilbook@talk21.com
**Opening hours**
Mon-Fri 9.15am – 5.30pm, Sat 9.30am
– 5.30pm

A good quality local bookshop with
a strong children's section.

## Waterstone's

| | |
|---|---|
| **Branch** | 121-125 Charing Cross Road London WC2H 0EA |
| **Tel** | 020 7434 4291 |
| **Fax** | 020 7437 3319 |

**Opening hours**
Mon-Sat 9.30am – 8pm, Sun noon – 6pm

| | |
|---|---|
| **Branch** | 203-206 Piccadilly London W1A 2AS |

| | |
|---|---|
| **Branch** | Whitgift Centre Croydon Surrey CR10 1UX |
| **Tel** | 020 8686 7032 |
| **Fax** | 020 8760 0638 |

**Opening hours**
Mon-Sat 9am – 6pm, Thurs 9am –
9pm, Sun 11am – 5pm

This new Waterstone's opening in
September 1999 will be Europe's
largest bookshop. Housed in the
old Simpson's department store on
Piccadilly, there will be seven floors
with a restaurant, cafés, magazines,
gifts and over 150,000 titles.

Meanwhile, the Waterstone's on
Charing Cross Road stands out
from the general pack for all the
right reasons.

Moving out of central London, the
branch in the Whitgift Centre has
been a cracking general bookshop –
it has an accomplished academic
department too – for a long time.
First as a Websters bookshop in the
'80s, then a Sherratt and Hughes
and finally a Waterstone's.

## West End Lane Books

| | |
|---|---|
| **Address** | 277 West End Lane West Hampstead London NW6 1QS |
| **Tel** | 020 7431 3770 |
| **Fax** | 020 7431 7655 |

**Opening hours**
Mon-Sat 10am – 7pm
**Services**
Events, readings

Founded to serve the bookish
residents of Hampstead. Although
essentially a general bookshop they
have strong pull towards spiritualism and philosophy and share the
premises with Darf Publishers, who
specialise in facsimile reprints of
out-of-print and rare books on the
Middle East and North Africa.

## Willesden Bookshop

| | |
|---|---|
| **Address** | Willesden Green Library Centre 95 High Road Willesden Green London NW10 4QU |
| **Tel** | 020 8451 7000 |
| **Fax** | 020 8830 1233 |

**Opening hours**
Mon-Fri 10am – 6pm, Sat 9.30am –
5.30pm
**Services**
Mail order, catalogues

An essential part of the Willesden library complex which also consists of a cinema, restaurant and conference facilities. It has a particularly good children's section, with a thoughtful range of multicultural titles. In keeping with its links to the Kilburn Bookshop (it is a sister outlet) the Irish, social studies and women's interest sections are well stocked.

## Wimbledon Books & Music

**Address**   58 Wimbledon Hill Road
London
SW19 7PA
**Tel**   020 8879 3101
**Fax**   020 8879 3101
**Email**
wim001@gardners-books.co.uk
**Opening hours**
Mon-Sat 9.30am – 6pm, Sun noon – 5pm

This oasis of books and music on Wimbledon's main shopping street is not far from Fielders. Since opening in 1996 they have firmly established themselves as a good-calibre bookshop and differentiate themselves from local competition by discounting the majority of books on offer – even new books and bestsellers. The classical music department is also worth a visit.

## Wordsworth Books

**Branch**   11 Butterfly Walk
Camberwell Green
London
SE5 8RW
**Tel**   020 7277 1377
020 7277 1168
**Opening hours**
Mon-Fri 9am – 7.30pm, Sat 9am – 6.30pm

**Branch**   116 Clapham High Street
London
SW4 7UH
**Tel**   020 7622 5344
**Opening hours**
Mon-Sat 9.30am – 6pm

**Branch**   19 Sidcup High Street
Sidcup
Kent
DA14 6HH
**Tel**   020 8309 5444
**Opening hours**
Mon-Sat 9am – 5.30pm

Fairly standard general bookshops providing a mix of new and bargain books to Camberwell, Sidcup and Clapham area.

## The Works

**Address**   Unit 2 Camden High Street
London
NW1
**Tel**   020 7284 3033
**Opening hours**
Mon-Fri 9am – 7pm, Sat 9am – 8pm, Sun 10am – 8pm

A general bargain bookshop located on busy Camden High Street. Most subject areas are covered and the books are keenly priced.

# ℒanguages

**Arabic • EFL • Esperanto • French • German • Greek Italian • Portuguese • Spanish**

## Alkitab Bookshop

**Address**   128c London Road
Kingston upon Thames
Surrey
KT2 6QJ
**Tel**   020 8549 4479
**Fax**   020 8549 4479

*See Countries*

## City Lit Bookshop

**Address**   City Lit
16 Stukeley Street
London
WC2B 5LJ
**Tel**   020 7405 3110
**Opening hours**
Mon-Fri 12pm – 7.30pm, Sat 12pm –
3pm

The City Literary Institute book-shop deals mainly with course texts associated with the wide range of courses on offer. Languages are a particular specialisation from major languages such as French, German and Spanish to Welsh and Cornish.

## Esperanto Bookshop

**Address**   140 Holland Park Avenue
London
W11 4UF
**Tel**   020 7727 7821
**Fax**   020 7229 5784
**Web**
www.esperanto.demon.co.uk
**Email**
eab@esperanto.demon.co.uk
**Opening hours**
Mon-Fri 9.30am – 6pm – 2.10pm

If you want to learn Esperanto this

is the place to come. Books and audiovisual learning aids, along with literature in the universal language that hasn't quite become universal.

## Eurocentre Bookshop

**Address**   21 Meadow Court
London
SE1 9EU
**Tel**   020 8318 5633
**Fax**   020 8318 9057
**Opening hours**
Mon-Fri 1pm – 2.10pm

English as a foreign language is the focus of this small bookshop catering for students within the Eurocentre.

## European Bookshop

**Address**   5 Warwick Street
London
W1R 6BH
**Tel**   020 7734 5259
**Fax**   020 7287 1720
**Email**
direct@esb.co.uk
**Opening hours**
Mon-Fri 9.30am – 6pm
**Services**
Mail order, catalogues

Originally named the Hachette Bookshop and founded in 1890, it was then devoted entirely to the French language. Since 1985, however, it has been expanded, renamed and is now one of the foremost language bookshops in London. Situated on the Soho side of Piccadilly Circus, it has a wide selection of fiction and non-fiction in French, German, Italian, Spanish and Portuguese as well as language courses covering the majority of European languages.

## French Bookseller Librairie La Page

**Address**   7 Harrington Road
South Kensington
London
SW7 3ES
**Tel**   020 7589 5991
**Fax**   020 7225 2662

*See Countries*

## Grant and Cutler

**Address**   55-57 Great Marlbourgh
Street
London
W1V 2AY
**Tel**   020 7734 2012
**Fax**   020 7734 9272
**Web**
www.grant-c.demon.co.uk
**Email**
postmaster@grant-c.demon.co.uk
**Opening hours**
Mon-Sat 9am – 5.30pm (Thurs 9am – 7pm)
**Services**
Mail order, catalogues

Feels more like a warehouse than a bookshop but it's a brilliant shop nonetheless. Founded in 1936, this is the UK's largest specialist foreign language bookseller. They specialise in French, German, Spanish, Italian, Portuguese and Russian but also cover more than 200 of the world's other languages. Most of the staff speak at least one foreign language and the range of stock is extensive with over 100,000 books, videos, CDs and multimedia items. They're easy to find just a short walk east from the top of Carnaby Street.

## Guru Books

**Address** 106 Drummond Street
London
NW1 2HN
**Tel** 020 7388 3939
**Opening hours**
By appointment only
**Services**
Mail order, catalogues

Specialises in books in the southern Asia language of Tamil. They are a mail order company but will accept visitors by appointment.

## Italian Bookshop

**Address** 7 Cecil Court
Charing Cross Road
London
WC2N 4EZ
**Tel** 020 7240 1634
**Fax** 020 7240 1635

*See Countries*

## KELTIC Bookshop

**Address** 25 Chepstow Corner
Chepstow Place
London
W2 4XE
**Tel** 020 7229 8560/8456
**Fax** 020 7221 7955
**Web**
www.keltic.co.uk
**Email**
shop@keltic-london.co.uk
**Opening hours**
Mon-Fri 10am – 5.30pm, Sat 10am –
5pm
**Services**
Mail order, catalogues

KELTIC or Kensington English Language Teaching and Information Centre is an English language specialist. Dealing in all aspect of English as a foreign language, for teachers and students alike, they have a massive range of textbooks, tapes, videos and computer software.

## LCL International Bookseller

**Address** 104/106 Judd Street
London
WC1H 9NF
**Tel** 020 7837 0486
**Fax** 020 7833 9452
**Email**
sales.lcl@btinternet.com
**Opening hours**
Mon-Fri 9am – 6pm, Sat 9.30am –
2.30pm
**Services**
Mail order, catalogues, events

Over 100 languages are represented here with language learning materials, dictionaries and literature by the hundred. The book stock is complemented by an equally impressive range of videos, cassettes and interactive language learning aids on CD-ROM. The shop has a demonstration area to sample videos and CD-ROM products and a whole floor dealing exclusively with English as a foreign language.

# Languages

## Linguaphone Language Centre

**Address**   124-126 Brompton Road
London
SW3 1JD
**Tel**   020 7589 2422
**Fax**   020 7584 7052
**Email**
langcent@linguaphone.co.uk
**Opening hours**
Mon-Sat 10am – 6pm

If you haven't seen the shop you've almost certainly seen the Linguaphone adverts in newspapers and magazines with their claim for a quick and easy path to fluency in the language of your choice. Founded around 80 years ago and situated opposite Harrods, this shop is devoted to language learning in the Linguaphone way. They publish their own courses and if you mention you heard about them in *The Bookshops of London* they will give you a 10% discount!

## OCS Japanese Books

**Address**   2 Grosvenor Parade
Uxbridge Road
Ealing
London
W5 3NN
**Tel**   020 8992 6335
**Fax**   020 8993 0891

*See Countries*

# *Literature*

**Bloomsbury Group • Classics • Dickens • Letters • Manuscripts**
**Modern First Editions • Poetry • Private Press • Signed Items**

## Bell Book and Radmall

**Address**  4 Cecil Court
Charing Cross Road
London
WC2N 4HE
**Tel**  020 7240 2161
**Fax**  020 7379 1062
**Email**
bellbr@dial.pipex.com
**Opening hours**
Mon-Fri 10am – 5.30pm, Sat 11am – 4pm
**Services**
Catalogues

Opened in 1974, they deal mainly
with first editions of modern
American and English literature.
Prices are on the high side, as befits
a shop selling rare items, but the
stock has quality and is invariably
in fine condition.

## Bertram Rota Ltd

**Address**  1st Floor
31 Long Acre
Covent Garden
London
WC2E 9LT
**Tel**  020 7836 0723
**Fax**  020 7499 9058
**Web**
www.ourworld.compuserve.com/home
page/bertramrota
**Email**
bertramrota@compuserve.com
**Opening hours**
Mon-Fri 9.30am – 5.30pm
**Services**
Catalogues, mail order

More akin to a private library than
a bookshop, but unlike a library
you can, wallet permitting, buy

# *Literature*

books here. Founded by Bertram Rota in 1923, his son Anthony and grandson Julian now run the business. The collection of first editions of English and American literature is simply superb. Private Press books, manuscripts, letters, signed items, corrected proofs and drawings of literary importance all feature strongly. Catalogues (four per year) are available on request and searches are undertaken for specific books.

## Bloomsbury Bookshop

**Address**   12 Bury Place
London
WC1A 2JL
**Tel**   020 7404 7433
**Opening hours**
Mon-Sat 11am – 6pm, Sun 1pm – 5pm

Delightful shop conducive to browsing located in the literary enclave off Southampton Row. On every visit you will feel that a literary treasure is just waiting to be discovered at the bottom of the next pile of books. The strongest subject areas are history, philosophy, literary criticism and the classics. The most comprehensive section is that on economic history.

## Bloomsbury Workshop

**Address**   12 Galen Place
London
WC1A 2JR
**Tel**   020 7405 0632
**Opening hours**
Mon-Fri 10am – 5.30pm

Can be found off Bury Place which is close to Bloomsbury Square. This gallery and bookshop specialises in the work of the celebrated Bloomsbury Group. Virginia Woolf, E.M. Forster, Leonard Woolf, Roger Fry, Vanessa Bell, Maynard Keynes, Duncan Grant, David Garnett, Lytton Strachey and Clive Bell are among the writers and artists whose first editions, paintings and drawings are available here.

## Dickens House Museum

**Address**   48 Doughty Street
London
WC1A 1LH
**Tel**   020 7405 2127
**Opening hours**
Mon-Sat 10am – 5pm

*See Museums & Galleries*

## R A Gekoski

**Address**   Pied Bull Yard
15a Bloomsbury Square
London
WC1A 2LP
**Tel**   020 7404 6676
**Fax**   020 7404 6595
**Opening hours**
Mon-Fri 10am – 5.30pm

A small, highly specialist stock of mainly modern first editions, letters and manuscripts are dispensed from an office-come-shop in this pleasant courtyard. The American proprietor is an avid football fan (he supports Coventry City) and the author of an illuminating work on a fan's eye view of a season in the Premiership.

## Heywood Hill

**Address** 10 Curzon Street
London
W1Y 7FJ
**Tel** 020 7629 0647
**Fax** 020 7408 0286
**Opening hours**
Mon-Fri 9am – 5.30pm, Sat 9am –
12.30pm
**Services**
Mail order

This Mayfair institution was founded in the '30s and boasted Nancy Mitford as a bookseller during the Second World War. The stock is made up of new, second-hand and antiquarian books displayed in a pleasingly genteel manner on polished wooden tables and groaning shelves. The emphasis is on literature, history, travel and biography and there is a chidren's department located in the basement. It's definitely one of literary London's treats to visit this ghost of bookselling past.

## John Sandoe Books

**Address** 10 Blacklands Terrace
Sloane Square
London
SW3 2SR
**Tel** 020 7589 9473
**Fax** 020 7581 2084
**Email**
books@jsandoe.demon.co.uk
**Opening hours**
Mon-Sat 9.30am – 5.30pm (Wed
9.30am – 7.30pm)
**Services**
Mail order, catalogues

Close to Sloane Square and the Kings Road, John Sandoe Books is one of the best-known independent bookshops in the capital. The three floors are crammed with books on literature and the arts in general. It has a style of its own and is the sort of bookshop that retains the loyalty of its customers even when they move out of the area, so reliable is its service and reputation.

## Marchmont Books

**Address** 39 Burton Street
London
WC1H 9AL
**Tel** 020 7387 7989

*See Secondhand*

## Nigel Williams Rare Books

**Address** 22 Cecil Court
London
WC2N 4HE
**Tel** 020 7836 7757
**Fax** 020 7379 5918
**Opening hours**
Mon-Sat 10am – 6pm

Specialising in 19th- and 20th-century first editions with a particular leaning towards classic detective fiction such as Conan Doyle and Agatha Christie. There is also a excellent collection of P.G. Wodehouse.

## Poetry Book Society

**Address** Book House
45 East Hill
London
SW18 2QZ

**Tel**      020 8870 8405
**Fax**     020 8877 1615
**Web**    www.poetrybooks.co.uk
**Email**   info@poetrybooks.co.uk
**Opening hours**
Mon-Fri 9.30am – 5.30pm
**Services**
Mail order, catalogues

Although not actually a bookshop, it is included in this guide because of its speciality. Founded by T.S. Eliot in 1953, it is a mail order company dedicated to promoting poetry around the world. Apart from offering general poetry books they also provide guidance to would-be poets. They were previously in Betterton Street, close to Covent Garden, where there was a good café, a bar and a poetry space downstairs that doubled as a club. This all fell to pieces and they had to relocate to Book House, their present home.

## Ulysses

**Address**  40 Museum Street
            London
            WC1A 1LT
**Tel**      020 7831 1600
**Fax**     020 7419 0070
**Web**
www.antiquarian.com/ulysses
**Email**
ulyssesbooks@fsbdial.co.uk
**Opening hours**
Mon-Sat 10.30am – 6pm, Sun noon – 6pm
**Services**
Mail order, catalogues

Glass cases, dark wood and lines of leather-bound books and 20th-century first editions populate this bookshop just over the road from the British Museum. The emphasis is on quality and the prices are subsequently high. Nevertheless, the regular catalogues of modern first editions always contain a wide spectrum of authors and prices. The newly established web site also boasts a database of over 10,000 books.

# Mind, Body & Spirit

**Acupuncture • Astrology • Exercise • Health • Herbalism**
**Homeopathy • New Age • Occult • Paranormal • Spiritualism • Tarot**

## Acumedic Centre

**Address**    101-105 Camden High
          Street
          London, NW1 7JN
**Tel**        020 7388 5783
**Email**
info@acumedic.com
**Opening hours**
Mon-Sat 9am – 6pm
**Services**
Mail order, catalogues

A renowned alternative health centre specialising in acupuncture and Chinese herbal therapy. The bookshop covers all aspects of health and authorised guides to acupuncture and Oriental medicine. Subjects covered include: osteopathy, homeopathy, herbalism, gemmology, physical exercise and t'ai chi. The health products side of the centre provides acupuncture equipment, homeopathic supplies and natural beauty products.

## Atlantis Bookshop

**Address**    49a Museum Street
          London
          WC1A 1LY
**Tel**        020 7405 2120
**Fax**        020 7430 0535
**Web**
www.atlantisbookshop.demon.co.uk
**Email**
books@atlantisbookshop.demon.co.uk
**Opening hours**
Mon-Sat 11am – 6pm
**Services**
Mail order, catalogues

New age and occult enthusiasts are

well catered for here. A large stock of new and secondhand books on witchcraft, astrology, spiritualism, paganism, psychic phenomena and the paranormal sits happily alongside a selection of tarot cards and crystal balls.

## Compendium Books

**Address**  234 High Street
Camden
London
NW1 8QS
**Tel**  020 7485 8944
020 7267 1525
**Fax**  020 7267 0193
**Web**
www.compendiumbooks.com
**Email**
compbks@dircom.co.uk
**Opening hours**
Mon-Wed 10am – 6pm, Thurs-Sat 10am – 7pm, Sun noon – 6pm

*See Politics & Social Sciences*

## Heal Services

**Address**  26 Clarendon Rise
London
SE13 4EY
**Tel**  020 8297 1661
**Opening hours**
Mon-Fri 8am – 5pm
**Services**
Mail order, catalogues

A highly specialised bookshop set up primarily to cater for the students of the nearby College Of Homeopathy. The range covers all aspects of the subject and caters for practitioners as well as students. They also have a small section on personal development.

## Minerva Homeopathic Books

**Address**  173 Fulham Palace Road
Hammersmith
London
W6 8QT
**Tel**  020 7385 1361
**Fax**  020 7385 0861
**Email**
minervabooks@aol.com
**Opening hours**
Mon-Fri 9.30am – 5.30pm
**Services**
Mail order, catalogues

Originally founded as a mail order service they now have their own shop specialising in homeopathic medicine, with a clinic attached, located just a few doors down from Charing Cross Hospital.

## Mysteries New Age Centre

**Address**  9-11 Monmouth Street
London
WC2H 6DA
**Tel**  020 7240 3688
**Fax**  020 7836 4679
**Opening hours**
Mon-Sat 10am – 6pm

Gives itself an apt description of 'London's Psychic and New Age Centre'. The host of paranormal, psychic and spiritual apparatus is all embracing: tarot cards, dowsing, crystal balls, pyramid energy, incense, pendulums, aural research, biorhythms, natural healing and remedies. The range of books to accompany the above is well ordered and easy to peruse. Readings of a psychic nature are available every day and courses are held on tarot reading, astrology, palmistry and spiritual guidance.

## Nutri Centre Bookshop

**Address**  Hale Clinic
7 Park Crescent
London
W1N 3HE
**Tel**  020 7323 2382
**Fax**  020 7636 0276
**Web**
www.nutricentre.co.uk
**Email**
eng@nutricentre.com
**Opening hours**
Mon-Fri 9am – 7pm, Sat 10am – 4.30pm
**Services**
Mail order, signings, catalogues, events

The Nutri Centre Bookshop is attached to the world-renowned Hale Clinic, which also houses a reference library. The centre is at the forefront of complementary medicine in the UK and is equipped with a bookshop stocking a wide range of books on maintaining a healthy mind, body and soul. They also offer a search service for hard-to-find American titles.

## Watkins Books

**Address**  19 Cecil Court
Charing Cross Road
London
WC2N 4EZ
**Tel**  020 7836 2182
**Fax**  020 7836 6700
**Web**
www.watkinsbooks.com

**Email**
service@watkinsbooks.com
**Opening hours**
Mon-Fri 10am – 6pm (Thurs 10am – 8pm), Sat 10.30am – 6pm
**Services**
Mail order, catalogues, signings

A long-established new age and occult specialist originally founded in 1895 by Geoffrey Watkins as a centre for the Theosophical Society – it's also claimed that Mozart once stayed the night on this very site, although that would have been well over 100 years before Watkins came into being! What is certain is that it is now perhaps one of the most famous esoteric bookshops in the world, with a varied range of new and secondhand books. Periodicals, magazines, videos and CDs from around the world complement the book stock.

## Wholefood Books

**Address**  24 Paddington Street
London
W1M 4DR
**Tel**  020 7935 3924
**Fax**  020 7486 2756
**Opening hours**
Mon 8.45am – 6pm, Tues-Fri 8.45am – 6.30pm, Sat 8.45am – 1pm

Perhaps the only place in the capital where you can buy organic fruit and vegetables and browse books at the same time. Mainly a health food store, there is also a range of books on health, alternative therapies, vitamins, organic farming, vegetarian cookery and natural childbirth.

## Wilde Ones

**Address**   283 Kings Road
London
SW3 5EW
**Tel**   020 7352 9531
**Fax**   020 7352 3844
**Web**
www.wildeones.com
**Email**
shop@wildeones.com
**Opening hours**
Mon-Fri 10am – 6pm, Sat 10am –
7pm, Sun noon – 7pm

**Services**
Mail order

The bookshop is only a small part
of this new age sanctuary located
on Kings Road. The shop is broadly
divided into two parts, one selling
books covering most new age
themes and the other selling all
manner of new age sundries from
Native American jewellery to
crystals. There is a small garden for
customers to relax in and also a
resident palmist and tarot reader.

# *Museums & Galleries*

**Archaeology • Art • Film & TV • Gardens • History • London Photography • Transport • War**

## British Museum Bookshop

**Address**  British Museum
Great Russell Street
London
WC1B 3DG
**Tel**  020 7323 8587/8422
**Fax**  020 7580 8699
**Web**
www.britishmuseumcompany.co.uk
**Opening hours**
Mon-Sat 10am – 5pm, Sun noon – 6pm
**Services**
Mail order, catalogues, events

The emphasis is firmly in line with that of the museum collections: archaeology, classical history, medieval studies and ancient civilisations are the main areas. There is a small selection of children's educa-tional books and a far more extensive choice of cards, prints and souvenirs. There are plans to relocate and expand the shop once the magnificent Great Court project is completed.

## Design Museum Bookshop

**Address**  Butlers Wharf
Shad Thames
London
SE1 2YD
**Tel**  020 7403 6933
**Fax**  020 7378 6540

*See Art & Design*

## Dickens House Museum

**Address**    48 Doughty Street
London
WC1A 1LH
**Tel**    020 7405 2127
**Opening hours**
Mon-Sat 10am – 5pm

The Dickens House Museum is the only remaining house in London once lived in by the great man himself. It was orginally opened by the Dickens Fellowship in 1925 and is a valuable source of income to the charity which owns the museum. There is a small range of stock, both antiquarian and modern, by and about Dickens and his times. It is a popular London attraction and there is also a selection of videos, posters, cards and assorted souvenirs.

## Geffrye Museum

**Address**    Kingsland Road
London
E2 8EA
**Tel**    020 7739 5893
**Fax**    020 7729 5647
**Opening hours**
Tues-Sat 10am – 5pm

A fascinating museum in the East End and the subject of significant improvement over recent years. The museum itself consists of rooms created in the style of a particular period with an emphasis on understanding domestic interiors. The small gift shop carries a selection of books on English interiors, furniture design and local history.

## Hayward Gallery Shop

**Address**    Hayward Gallery
South Bank Centre
Belvedere Road
London
SE1 8SX
**Tel**    020 7960 5210
**Opening hours**
Mon-Sun 10am – 6pm

A specialist stock on individual artists from A to Z, photography, art reference, sculpture and contemporary art along with a comprehensive selection of publications and catalogues related to current exhibitions. Other products include a wide selection of cards, posters, calendars and gift items. It's fair to say that the South Bank Centre is not the most attractive of environments but the bookshop at least provides some respite from the concrete walls outside.

## ICA Bookshop

**Address**    28 Nash House
The Mall
London
SW1Y 5AH
**Tel**    020 7925 2434

*See Art & Design*

## Imperial War Museum

**Address**    Lambeth Road
London
SE1 6HZ
**Tel**    020 7416 5000
**Opening hours**
Mon-Sun 10am – 6pm

*See Transport & Military*

## London Transport Museum

**Address**  The Piazza
Covent Garden
London
WC2E 7BB
**Tel**  020 7379 6344
**Opening hours**
Mon Sun 10am – 6pm

*See Transport & Military*

## Museum of Garden History

**Address**  Lambeth Palace Road
London
SE1 7LB
**Tel**  020 7261 1891
**Fax**  020 7401 8869

*See Crafts & Pastimes*

## Museum of London

**Address**  150 London Wall
London
EC2Y 5HN
**Tel**  020 7600 3699
**Opening hours**
Mon-Sat 10am – 5.50pm, Sun noon – 5.50pm

Located in the City, close to the Barbican Centre and five minutes walk from St Paul's Cathedral. In the bookshop at the entrance to the museum there is a comprehensive collection of books relating to the history of London and its people. The books cover all aspects of London life, from maps and guides to specialist titles on the collections in the museum. Children's requirements are met handsomely with a well-chosen set of educational and activity books. Gifts, stationery and music with a London theme tempt the visitor.

## Museum of the Moving Image Bookshop

**Address**  South Bank
London
SE1 8XT
**Tel**  020 7928 3535
**Fax**  020 7815 1378

*See Performing Arts*

## National Army Museum Shop

**Address**  Royal Hospital Road
Chelsea
London
SW3 4HT
**Tel**  020 7730 0717
**Fax**  020 7823 6573
**Opening hours**
Mon-Sun 10am – 5.30pm

*See Transport & Military*

## National Gallery Bookshop

**Address**  National Gallery
Trafalgar Square
London
WC2N 5DN
**Tel**  020 7747 2870
**Opening hours**
Mon-Sat 10am – 5.30pm (Wed 10am – 8.30pm), Sun noon – 6pm

The main National Gallery shop is located in the Sainsbury Wing. Along with the expected range of cards, prints, stationery and gifts there is an impressive collection of exhibition catalogues and art books.

## National Portrait Gallery

**Address**  St Martin's Place
London
WC2H 0HE
**Tel**  020 7306 0055
**Opening hours**
Mon-Fri 10am – 6pm, Sun noon – 6pm

The extensive range of books and merchandise reflects the magnificent art collections of the gallery. National Portrait Gallery publications, British art and portraits, art history and biography are the major areas of expertise. There is a selection of literature and children's educational books, including tapes and videos. Posters, postcards, cards and stationery depicting the famous images within the gallery are also available. The range of crafts is of interest to the art lover and tourist alike, with bags, jigsaws, bookends, mugs and other gift items crammed into this gallery shop.

## Natural History Museum Bookshop

**Address**  Natural History Museum
Cromwell Road
London
SW7 5BD
**Tel**  020 7938 9022
**Fax**  020 7938 8880
**Opening hours**
Mon-Sat 10am – 5.45pm, Sun 11am – 5.45pm

*See Environment & Nature*

## Photographer's Gallery Bookshop

**Address**  5/8 Great Newport Street
London
WC2H 7HY
**Tel**  020 7831 1772
**Opening hours**
Mon-Sat 11am – 6pm, Sun noon – 6pm
**Services**
Mail order

*See Art & Design*

## Pollock's Toy Museum

**Address**  1 Scala Street
London
W1P 1CT
**Tel**  020 7636 3452
**Opening hours**
Mon-Sat 10am – 5pm

The museum was founded in the '50s with the toy theatre collection inherited from Benjamin Pollock, the last of the Victorian toy theatre makers and printers. It is adjacent to a toy shop and only minutes from Goodge Street underground, making it a convenient location to take children to when they've tired of other, more publicised attractions. The shop can be entered without going into the museum but don't miss one of the most unusual and fascinating collections in London. There is a small range of books on dolls, toys and collectables with some children's books.

## RA Bookshop

**Address**   Royal Academy of Arts
Burlington House
Piccadilly
London
W1V ODS
**Tel**       020 7439 7438
**Fax**       020 7434 0837

*See Art & Design*

## Science Museum

**Address**   Ottakar's
Exhibition Road
South Kensington
London
SW7 2DD
**Tel**       020 7938 8255
**Fax**       020 7938 8127
**Opening hours**
Mon-Sun 10am – 6pm

Once a Dillons-run store, it is now run by Ottakar's and is generally a better shop for it. The focus, however, remains entirely on all aspects of science and technology, covering both popular and specialist fields. General subjects are well represented and the children's section is biased towards practical activities and basic science topics.

## Serpentine Gallery Bookshop

**Address**   Kensington Gardens
London
W2 3XA
**Tel**       020 7298 1502
**Fax**       020 7402 4103
**Email**
bookshop@serpentinegallery.org
**Opening hours**

Mon-Sun 10am – 6pm

In the often overlooked Serpentine Gallery you will find this equally commendable bookshop concentrating on contemporary art in all its forms.

## Tate Gallery Bookshop

**Address**   Millbank
London
SW1 4RY
**Tel**       020 7887 8008
**Opening hours**
Mon Sun 10.30am – 5.30pm

The range of books here reflects the collections at the Tate – both permanent and temporary exhibitions – and includes all aspects of art throughout the ages. British painting from 1570 to the present and foreign 20th-century painting and sculpture are the main attractions. There are always displays of catalogues, books and other items relating to special exhibitions and events in the gallery. Prints, posters, slides, cards and gifts are included in the repertoire.

## V & A Bookshop

**Address**   V & A Museum
Cromwell Road
South Kensington
London
SW7 2RL
**Tel**       020 7938 8434
**Fax**       020 7988 8623
**Opening hours**
Mon noon – 5.30pm, Tues-Sun 10am – 5.30pm

After a walk around this stupendous museum, spend some time in the equally excellent shop. The books cover the study, conservation and preservation of the major collections in the V & A: textiles, ceramics, furniture, metalwork, sculpture and the arts and crafts of the Far East, Indian and Islamic cultures. Books form only part of what is a gift-givers delight and the annual V & A Christmas catalogue is always a pleasure to receive.

## Wallace Collection

**Address**   Hertford House
Manchester Square
London
W1M 6BN
**Tel**   020 7935 0687
**Fax**   020 7224 2155
**Web**
www.demon.co.uk/heritage/wallace
**Email**
trade@wallcoll.demon.co.uk
**Opening hours**
Mon-Sat 10am – 5pm, Sun 2pm – 5pm
**Services**
Mail order, catalogues

Hertford House was the town house of Sir Richard Wallace whose widow left the contents to the nation after his death in 1897 – the collection opened as a museum three years later. The shop was modified in 1994 and specialises in books on the fine and decorative art of 18th-century France. The museum plans to celebrate its centenary in 2000 by opening new basement galleries, educational facilities and a restaurant.

## Zwemmer

**Address**   Whitechapel Art Gallery
Whitechapel High Street
London
E1 7QX
**Tel**   020 7247 6924

*See Art & Design*

# Performing Arts

**Cinema • Dance • Drama • Music • Opera • Stage Television • Theatre**

## Barbican Music Shop

**Address**    Cromwell Tower
          Barbican
          London
          EC2Y 8DD
**Tel**         020 7588 9242
**Fax**        020 7628 1080
**Opening hours**
Mon-Fri 9am – 5.30pm, Sat 8.45am – 4pm

Stocks a reasonable range of books on classical and popular music together with a comprehensive selection of scores. There are many titles on how to play instruments and more serious tomes for students of music at the nearby Guildhall School of Music and Drama.

## H Baron

**Address**    76 Fortune Green Road
          London
          NW6
**Tel**         020 7794 4041
**Opening hours**
Fri-Sat 1pm – 6pm

A limited opening period means you have to be determined to make a visit. The stock consists of second-hand and rare books and musical scores.

## BBC Shop

**Address**    Broadcasting House
          Portland Place
          London
          W1A 1AA
**Tel**         020 7765 0025

**Opening hours**
Mon-Sun 9.30am – 6pm

Home to the corporation's retailing arm and packed with BBC books, tapes and videos destined to bring back memories of your favourite programme. Cards, posters, and all manner of gifts are here. Combine an organised tour of the BBC building with a trip to the shop.

## BBC World Service Shop

**Address**   Bush House
              Strand
              London
              WC2 4PH
**Tel**       020 7557 2576
**Fax**       020 7240 4811
**Email**
worldservice.shop@bbc.co.uk
**Opening hours**
Mon-Fri 10am – 6pm, Sat 10am – 5.30pm

The BBC World Service started this shop as an information centre for listeners and has watched it grow into a profitable contributor to BBC coffers. It is at street level at the entrance to Bush House facing King's College. Here is the full range of BBC publications with tapes and videos supplying a nostalgic trip through the TV and radio of yesteryear. Current programmes are covered equally well. The World Service is a lifeline for many people around the world and here you can obtain, free of charge, leaflets in the languages of the countries in which programmes are received, detailing the all-important frequencies for reception. A selection of short-wave radios puts the average Dixons to shame. This is a fine example of a part of the BBC that provides an invaluable service but unless you have cause to search for it you may never know it exists.

## Books etc

**Address**   Level 2
              Royal Festival Hall
              South Bank Centre
              London
              SE1 8XX
**Tel**       020 7620 0403
**Fax**       020 7620 0426
**Opening hours**
Mon-Sun 11am – 10pm

Situated in the centre of the Festival Hall with a range of books to reflect the artisitic and literary nature of events in the South Bank complex. The shop is small but still manages to carry an impressive range of general new titles and paperback fiction.

## Books and Lyrics

**Address**   Merton Abbey Mills
              Watermill Way
              London
              SW19 2RD
**Tel**       020 8543 0625
**Opening hours**
Tues-Sun 10am – 6pm

Part of the diverse Merton Abbey centre offering a good general range of secondhand books with a bias towards music titles, sheet music and a selection of vinyl.

## Boosy and Hawkes Music Shop

**Address**  295 Regent Street
London
W1R 8JH
**Tel**  020 7580 2060
**Opening hours**
Mon-Fri 9am – 6pm, Sat 10am – 4pm

A business with an illustrious history in the music world. In 1990 the interior was destroyed by fire and then reopened the following year fully restored to its 1930s art deco splendour, originally designed by Anna Zinkeisen. It is the only company in the world to combine instrument manufacturing with a leading music publishing business and the shop carries every piece of music in the Boosey and Hawkes catalogue currently in print. There is a wide selection of printed music and music books from all the leading publishers. The stock is more eclectic than it once was, and although it concentrates on classical music and education there is an enhanced section on popular and contemporary music. Also on sale is a comprehensive selection of periodicals, stationery, gift items and accessories.

## Chappells of Bond Street

**Address**  50 New Bond Street
London
W1Y 9HA
**Tel**  020 7491 2777
**Fax**  020 7491 0133
**Opening hours**

Mon-Fri 9.30am – 6pm, Sat 9.30am – 5pm

A huge range of sheet music and how-to-play guides alongside a host of musical instruments.

## Cinema Bookshop

**Address**  13 Great Russell Street
London
WC1B 3NH
**Tel**  020 7637 0206
**Fax**  020 7436 9979
**Opening hours**
Mon-Sat 10.30am – 5.30pm

A movie fan's dream with all aspects of the silver screen covered in this little store absolutely overflowing with items of interest to film buffs. Crammed packed with books new and old they also carry posters, assorted memorabilia and signed photographs of movie stars from the golden age of Hollywood to the modern-day heroes like Brad Pitt and Leonardo Di Caprio.

## Cinema Store

**Address**  4b Orion House
Upper St Martins Lane
London
WC2
**Tel**  020 7379 7838
**Opening hours**
Mon-Wed, Sat 10am – 6pm, Thurs, Fri 10am – 7pm, Sun noon – 6pm

A glitzy store specialising in anything and everything connected to the cinema past and present, with new books, a huge stock of magazines, videos, posters, cards and a host of other items linked to film.

## Dance Books

**Address**   15 Cecil Court
St Martins Lane
London
WC2N 4EZ
**Tel**   020 7836 2314
**Fax**   020 7497 0473
**Opening hours**
Mon-Sat 11am – 7pm

Founded in the mid-'60s by John O'Brien, an ex-Ballet Rambert dancer, so no shortage of expertise and first-hand knowledge here. The shop is attractively decorated with dance prints and the stock is well organised. All forms of dance and human movement are covered by the well-chosen range of new and secondhand books, with some bargains to be found. There are also a number of dance videos on offer.

## David Drummond

**Address**   11 Cecil Court
Charing Cross Road
London
WC2N
**Tel**   020 7836 1142
**Opening hours**
Mon-Fri 11am – 5.45pm

David Drummond has been operating here since the late '60s and claims that 'interest in the theatre manifested itself Frankenstein-like to the detriment of my performing career'. Over 5,000 books on the performing arts and juvenilia pre-1940s with a bias towards Victorian and illustrated books. There is a wide selection of playbills, cards and picture postcards.

## Dress Circle

**Address**   57 Monmouth Street
Covent Garden
London
WC2H 9DG
**Tel**   020 7240 2227
**Fax**   020 7379 8540
**Web**
www.dresscircle.co.uk
**Email**
online@dresscircle.co.uk
**Opening hours**
Mon-Sat 10am – 7pm

'The Greatest Showbiz Shop in the World' is packed with soundtracks, memorabilia, theatre and film posters, scripts and musical scores. There is also a selection of books on all things celluloid and theatrical, particularly biographies of stars past and present.

## ENO Shop

**Address**   31 St Martins Lane
London
WC2N 4ER
**Tel**   020 7240 0270
**Web**
www.mdcmusic.co.uk
**Email**
classic@mdcmusic.co.uk
**Opening hours**
Mon 10am – 6pm, Tues-Sat 10am – 7.30pm

Although now owned by the MDC Classic Music group this specialist outlet is still referred to as the ENO (English National Opera) shop. CDs and tapes are in abundance and there is a nice choice of books – no sheet music though – on classical music and opera.

## The Folk Shop

**Address**    Cecil Sharp House
2 Regent's Park Road
London
NW1 7AY
**Tel**    020 7485 2206
**Opening hours**
Tues-Fri 9am – 5pm
**Services**
Mail order, magazine, library, catalogues

Cecil Sharp House is the home of the English Folk Dance and Song Society. There is a wide range of world music on tape, records and CD accompanied by books on customs, folklore, folk music and musicians.

## French's Theatre Bookshop

**Address**    52 Fitzroy Street
Fitrovia
London
W1P 6JR
**Tel**    020 7255 4300
**Fax**    020 7387 2161
**Web**
www.samuelfrench-london.co.uk
**Email**
theatre@samuelfrench-london.co.uk
**Opening hours**
Mon-Fri 9.30am – 5.30pm, Sat 11am – 5pm
**Services**
Mail order, catalogues

Samuel French was founded in 1830 as a publisher and the bookshop was opened in 1840. The shop has moved all over London but is now firmly settled just two minutes from Warren Street underground.

They have a huge selection of plays and general books on the theatre. The sections are clearly labelled and logically organised making it easy and enjoyable to find the book of your choice. They also keep an amazing selection of sound effects and dialect recordings.

## Helter Skelter

**Address**    4 Denmark Street
London
WC2H 8LL
**Tel**    020 7836 1151
**Fax**    020 7240 9880
**Web**
www.skelter.demon.co.uk
**Email**
helter@skelter.demon.co.uk
**Opening hours**
Mon-Fri 10am – 7pm, Sat 10am – 6pm
**Services**
Mail order, signings, catalogues, events

This site was originally the Regent Sound Recording Studios where the likes of the Rolling Stones recorded some of their early hits. Now it plays host to a dedicated rock music bookstore and associated ephemera.

## Kensington Music Shop

**Address**    9 Harrington Road
South Kensington
London, SW7 3ES
**Tel**    020 7589 9054
**Fax**    020 7225 2662
**Email**
kensingtonmusic@compuserve.com
**Opening hours**
Mon-Fri 9am – 5.30pm, Sat 9am – 4pm

**Services**
Mail order, catalogues

Located in the heart of London's museum district, this shop is found just a short stroll from the Royal College of Music and deals exclusively in books on music.

## Museum of the Moving Image Bookshop

**Address**    South Bank
London
SE1 8XT
**Tel**    020 7928 3535
**Fax**    020 7815 1378
**Opening hours**
Mon-Sun 10am – 9pm

A museum hugely popular with visitors to London, children and all those interested in film, TV and the media in general. The shop carries a variety of merchandise to attract the souvenir buyer and the books cover the specialist areas comprehensively, from animation to special effects and writing screenplays.

## National Film Theatre Bookshop

**Address**    National Film Theatre
South Bank
London
SE1 8XT
**Tel**    020 7928 3535
**Opening hours**
Mon-Sun 10am – 9pm

Located inside the National Film Theatre is this pleasant shop with a broad selection of books on and about all aspects of film. All NFT publications are stocked and there are also videos and cards. After visiting the shop for a screenplay or a technical book on cinematography relax in the café overlooking the Thames.

## Offstage Theatre and Film Bookshop

**Address**    37 Chalk Farm Road
London
NW1 8AJ
**Tel**    020 7485 4996
**Fax**    020 7916 8046
**Email**
offstage@btinternet.com
**Opening hours**
Mon-Sun 10am – 6pm
**Services**
Mail order

Located close to busy Camden market this specialist bookshop houses a wide range of new and secondhand books on the performing arts. Not quite as established as *The Mousetrap*, it has, however, been in existence for nearly 20 years. Drama, the media, film, criticism, biographies and stagecraft are well represented. A fascinating range of memorabilia with a large selection of theatre programmes provides good dreaming potential. Offstage also stocks technical books on make-up, lighting, sound and production. Whether you are a student of the arts or an avid theatregoer you will find something of interest here.

## Ray's Jazz Shop

**Address**   180 Shaftesbury Avenue
London
WC2H 8JS
**Tel**   020 7240 3969
**Opening hours**
Mon-Sat 10am – 6.30pm, Sun 2pm –
5pm

Ray was manager of the now
defunct Collets Jazz and Folk
Record Shop for 25 years before he
set up this landmark of the London
jazz scene. Records, CDs and tapes
are the mainstay and although the
book stock is small and largely
displayed behind the main counter,
it is completely in keeping with the
jazz specialisation.

## Royal National Theatre Bookshop

**Address**   Ground Floor Foyer
South Bank
London
SE1 9PX
**Opening hours**
Mon-Sat 10am – 11pm

The stock concentrates on the
theatre in general and items related
to the current repertoire, along with
a few other more general books.
There are play texts, especially
those of current London produc-
tions, critiques, biographies and
reference books. The remainder of
the stock is carefully chosen to
reflect the taste and interests of the
clientele and consists of literary
fiction and film and TV tie-ins.
Other products include quality
National Theatre branded products.

## Royal Shakespeare Company Shop

**Address**   Barbican Centre
London
EC2Y 8DS
**Tel**   020 7628 3351
**Opening hours**
From 6.15pm before performances

There are two bookstalls, one
located at the stalls level and the
other on level zero. There is the
expected range of Shakespeare texts
and books on drama, along with
Royal Shakespeare Society branded
merchandise.

## Stage Door Prints

**Address**   9 Cecil Court
Charing Cross Road
London
WC2N 4EZ
**Tel**   020 7240 1683
**Fax**   020 7379 5598
**Opening hours**
Mon-Fri 11am – 6pm, Sat 11.30am –
6pm

This is largely a print shop specialising in performance arts but there is
a modest range of books on opera,
music, ballet, theatre and film. The
range of ephemera and memorabilia
offers much of interest and there is
always a selection of autographed
photographs of Hollywood legends.

## Travis and Emery

**Address**   17 Cecil Court
Charing Cross Road
London
WC2N 4EZ
**Tel**   020 7240 2129

**Fax**       020 7497 0473
**Opening hours**
Mon-Sat 10am – 6pm

'Exclusively Music' proclaims the sign in the window but whether this is to deter from entry the more general browsers sampling the wealth of bookshops in Cecil Court, or a sales pitch, is unclear. Inside there are new and secondhand books on all aspects of music and specialist catalogues are issued. The collection of sheet music is extensive with prints and photographs as a variation to the theme.

# Vintage Magazine Shop

**Address**   39-41 Brewer Street
London
W1R 3FD
**Tel**       020 7439 8525
**Opening hours**
Mon-Thurs 10am – 8pm, Fri, Sat 10am – 10pm, Sun noon – 8pm

Deep in the heart of Soho, Vintage offers a small selection of cinema and theatre books, but they concentrate mainly on old magazines – of which there is a huge range – and stage and film posters. There is a selection of music press dating from the '70s that makes for interesting and nostalgic reading. Posters, cards and calendars complement the main stock.

# Politics & Social Sciences

**Black Writing • Economics • Gender • Irish Studies**
**Marxism • Pacifism • Politics • Socialism • Women's Studies**

## Bookmarks

**Address**  1 Bloomsbury Street
London
WC1B 3QE
**Tel**  020 7637 1848
**Fax**  020 7637 3416
**Opening hours**
Mon 12pm – 8pm, Tues-Fri 10am –
8pm, Sat 10am – 6pm, Sun 12pm –
6pm

Founded in the '60s as a mail order
service for the International
Socialists, they opened a bookshop
in the next decade and have since
grown substantially. They carry a
wide range of books on socialist
politics, lesbian and gay issues,
trade unionism, Marxism, social
sciences and black interest in a
bright new shop at the southern end
of Bloomsbury Street. The
Bookmark Club offers the best
socialist books at reduced prices (a
newsletter reviewing books is
produced regularly), ranging from
current issues and socialist fiction to
history and Marxist theory. A children's book catalogue is available
listing a selection from picture
books to teenage fiction: the
prevailing criteria are multicultural-
ism and anti-sexism.

## Centerprise Bookshop

**Address**  136 Kingsland High Street
Dalston
London
E8 2NS
**Tel**  020 7254 9632/9207
**Fax**  020 7923 1951

**Opening hours**
Mon-Fri 9.30am – 6pm, Sat 10am –
5.30pm

Centreprise is a community centre
located in the heart of Hackney and
has been a valuable resource for
local people for close on 25 years.
Books of a radical and political
nature are well represented alongside education, welfare issues, legal
rights, black issues, women's studies
and children's books along with a
more general selection including
fiction. The bookshop supports an
active local publishing scene and
there is an equally inventive
programme of arts and literature
events.

# Compendium Books

| | |
|---|---|
| **Address** | 234 High Street |
| | Camden |
| | London |
| | NW1 8QS |
| **Tel** | 020 7485 8944 |
| | 020 7267 1525 |
| **Fax** | 020 7267 0193 |

**Web**
www.compendiumbooks.com
**Email**
compbks@dircom.co.uk
**Opening hours**
Mon-Wed 10am – 6pm, Thurs-Sat
10am – 7pm, Sun noon – 6pm
**Services**
Mail order, signings, catalogues, events

A Pandora's box of delights in
Camden for the browser and buyer
alike. At the heart of so-called 'radical' bookselling since it opened in
1968, they have a great collection
of new age books, from the occult

to health, and excellent large
sections on women's studies,
current social issues, philosophy,
politics and world religions.

# Economist Bookshop

| | |
|---|---|
| **Address** | Clare Market |
| | Portugal Street |
| | London |
| | WC2A 2AB |
| **Tel** | 020 7405 5531 |
| **Fax** | 020 7403 1584 |

**Opening hours**
Mon-Fri 9am – 7pm (Wed 9am –
9.30pm), Sat 9.30am – 6pm

Occupying the middle ground of
LSE territory, students need go no
further for books on politics,
economics and social sciences.
Apart from the full range of new
titles there is always a wide selection of secondhand course and textbooks and basic reading for
students.

# Freedom Press Bookshop

| | |
|---|---|
| **Address** | Angel Alley |
| | 84b Whitechapel High Street |
| | London |
| | E1 7QX |
| **Tel** | 020 7247 9249 |
| **Fax** | 020 7377 9526 |

**Opening hours**
Mon-Fri 10.30am – 6pm, Sat 11am –
5pm

Located at the offices of anarchist
publisher Freedom Press, who for
the last 100 years have produced
and distributed alternative social
and political literature. There are
books, pamphlets and periodicals

here that you won't find in any other political bookshop along with other books on politics and the social sciences.

## Housemans

**Address**  5 Caledonian Road
London
N1 9DX
**Tel**  020 7837 4473
**Fax**  020 7278 0444
**Email**
100614.322@compuserve.com
**Opening hours**
Mon-Sat 10am – 6.30pm

Above the aptly named Porcupine Bookcellar and a short distance from King's Cross station. As an antidote to the military specialists elsewhere there is a substantial section here on pacifism and anti-militarism. In the politics section you can find books on anarchism alongside a large selection of political magazines and journals. The general books reflect the overall radical theme and include feminism, gay issues, the environment and contemporary fiction.

## Index Bookcentre

**Address**  16 Electric Avenue
London
SW9 8HY
**Tel**  020 7274 8342
**Fax**  020 7274 8351
**Email**
indexbookcentre@interramp.co.uk
**Opening hours**
Mon-Sat 10am – 6pm
**Services**
Mail order, events, signings, readings

Five years ago Index had two branches in London, one in Charlotte Street W1 and the other in Atlantic Road SW9. They have since been overtaken on the specialist front by outlets such as Bookmarks but the new site in Electric Avenue is still worth a visit. Socialist politics and history is the main theme with black writing, African and Caribbean topics well covered too. The range of general subjects is reasonable and affordable, with paperbacks in the majority. Local schools and libraries are supplied and this is reflected in the selection of textbooks and educational titles.

## John Buckle

**Address**  170 Wandsworth Road
London
SW8 2LA
**Tel**  020 7627 0599
**Web**
www.rcpbml.org.uk
**Email**
jbbooks@lineone.net
**Opening hours**
Mon-Sat 10am – 6pm
**Services**
Mail order, catalogues

New political and communist literature makes up the bulk of a stock range with a progressive profile.

## Kilburn Bookshop

**Address**  8 Kilburn Bridge
Kilburn High Road
London
NW6 6HT
**Tel**  020 7328 7071

**Fax**    020 7372 6474
**Opening hours**
Mon-Sat 10am – 6pm
**Services**
Mail order

Opened in 1985, this is a small shop situated on the Kilburn High Road opposite the junction with Belsize Road. They offer a broad range of fiction and non fiction, with a focus on Irish studies, black literature, new age topics and gay and lesbian titles standing out among the more general ranges.

# Parliamentary Bookshop

**Address**    12 Bridge Street
Parliament Square
London
SW1A 2JK
**Tel**    020 7219 3890
**Fax**    020 7219 3866
**Web**
www.parliament.uk
**Email**
bookshop@parliament.uk
**Opening hours**
Mon-Thurs 9.30am – 5.30pm, Fri 9am – 4pm
**Services**
Mail order

Opened in 1992 in order to provide better public access to the workings of Parliament, the shop is run by House of Commons staff who are able to provide knowledgeable information and advice. They stock parliamentary papers and official publications and a selection of books and periodicals on current affairs and the political scene.

# Pathfinder Bookshop

**Address**    47 The Cut
London
SE1 8LL
**Tel**    020 7401 2409
**Opening hours**
Mon 4pm – 6pm, Tues-Thurs 5pm – 7pm, Fri 4pm – 7pm, Sat 10am – 6pm
**Services**
Mail order

The premises has been a distribution point for Pathfinder Press for over 20 years and has been a bookshop since 1990. It is one of many similar shops around the world and is opposite the Old Vic Theatre, five minutes from Waterloo. The shop is staffed by volunteers and provides essential reading for those who want to understand and change the world. The stock is small at around 2,000 titles and covers socialist politics, books on the struggle for freedom and social justice and liberation movements. The writings of all great revolutionaries are available – Guevara, Trotsky, Marx, James Connelly *et al*. Discounts on Pathfinder's own titles can be had for members of the Pathfinder Readers Club.

# Politicos

**Address**    8 Artillery Row
Westminster
London
SW1P 1PZ
**Tel**    020 7828 0010
**Fax**    020 7828 8111
**Web**
www.politicos.co.uk
**Email**

politicos@artillery-row.demon.co.uk

**Opening hours**
Mon-Fri 9am – 6.30pm, Sat 10am –
6pm, Sun 11am – 5pm

**Services**
Events, mail order, catalogues, signings

Sportpages Bookshop off Charing
Cross Road has a TV showing live
sporting action and Politicos tempts
you in with live coverage of
proceedings in the House. This
bookshop was opened by the
former lobbyist Iain Dale and
boasts an unrivalled collection of
political books, both new and
secondhand, of every hue. There are
also gift items and a relaxing café
upstairs.

## Porcupine Bookcellar

**Address**    The Basement
                5 Caledonian Road
                London
                N1 9DX
**Tel**        020 7837 4473
**Opening hours**
Mon-Sat 10am – 6pm

The basement of Housemans
contains a general range of secondhand books with a slightly less
radical theme than the bookshop
above.

## Silver Moon

**Address**    64-68 Charing Cross Road
                London
                WC2H 0BB
**Tel**        020 7836 7906
**Fax**        020 7379 1018
**Email**
smwb@silvermoonbookshop.co.uk
**Opening hours**

Mon-Sat 10am – 6.30pm (Thurs 10am-
8), Sun noon – 6pm

**Services**    Mail order, signings,
catalogues, events

Jane Cholmeley and Sue
Butterworth started this business in
1984 and it has since grown to
occupy the two shops next door.
Silver Moon is now Europe's largest
women's bookshop, with close to
10,000 books of women's literature
and non-fiction by and about
women. They also have the best
lesbian selection in the country.
Women's music on CD and tape is
also stocked.

## Stationery Office

**Address**    123 Kingsway
                London
                WC2B 6PQ
**Tel**        020 7430 1671
**Fax**        020 7831 1326
**Opening hours**
Mon-Fri 9am – 5.30pm, Sat 10am –
3pm

*See Business*

## Woburn Bookshop

**Address**    10 Woburn Walk
                London
                WC1H 0JL
**Tel**        020 7388 7278
**Opening hours**
Mon-Fri 11am – 6pm, Sat 11am – 5pm

Mainly secondhand academic
books in the subject areas of social
sciences, politics, history and black
culture. It's a sister shop to
Porcupine Bookcellar in the
basement of Housemans.

# Notes

# Religion & Theology

**Buddhism • Catholicism • Christianity • Eastern Religions Islam • Judaism • Sufism**

## Aisenthal

**Address**   11 Ashbourne Parade
Finchley Road
London
NW11 OAD
**Tel/Fax**   020 8455 0501
**Opening hours**
Mon-Fri 9am – 6pm, Sun 9.30am –
2pm
**Services**
Mail order, catalogues

Right in the heart of London's
Jewish community, Aisenthal has
been owned and run by the same
family for over 35 years. Stocks a
wide selection of books in English
and Hebrew covering all aspects of
Judaica plus other gifts.

## Al-Noor Bookshop

**Address**   82 Park Road
London
NW1 4SH
**TelFax/**   020 7723 5414
*See Countries*

## Ark Christian Bookshop

**Address**   19 Pier Road
Erith
Dartford
Kent
DA8 1TA
**Tel**   01322 332515
**Opening hours**
Mon-Sat 9am – 5pm (Thurs closed)
**Services**
Mail order

The usual array of books about

Christianity can be found here.

## Bible Bookshop

**Address**   27 Clements Road
Ilford
Essex
IG1 1BH
**Tel/Fax**   020 8478 3278
**Opening hours**
Mon-Wed 9am – 5.15pm, Fri, Sat 9am
– 6pm

## Book Aid

**Address**   Mayeswood Road
Grove Park
London
SE12 9RP
**Tel**   020 8857 7794
**Fax**   020 8653 6577
**Opening hours**
Thurs only 9.30am – 8pm

A mainly Christian bookshop, which is an offshoot of the real mission that involves the shipping of Christian books and bibles to the world's needy areas. They have some 18,000 titles in stock but only a small proportion don't fit into the Christianity bracket.

## Books for Life

**Address**   Bethnal Green Mission
305 Cambridge Heath Road
London
E2 9LH
**Tel**   020 7729 4286
**Fax**   020 7729 4286
**Opening hours**
Mon-Fri 9.30am – 5.30pm, Sat 9.30am
– 12.30pm

Opposite the Museum of

Childhood in Bethnal Green and specialising in all aspects of Christianity.

## Bookstore Kingsway International Christian Centre

**Address**   411a Brixton Road
London
SW9 7DG
**Tel**   020 7733 8333
**Opening hours**
Mon-Sat 9.30am – 6pm

A substantial stock of books, videos and tapes all on a Christian theme.

## Canaan Christian Book Centre

**Address**   121 High Street
Staines
Middlesex
TW18 4PD
**Tel**   01784 457194
**Fax**   01784 441040
**Opening hours**
Mon-Thurs 9.30am – 5pm, Fri 9am – 5.30pm, Sat 9am – 5pm

## Carmel Gifts

**Address**   62 Edgware Way
Edgware
Middlesex
HA8 8JS
**Tel**   020 8958 7632
**Fax**   020 8958 6226
**Opening hours**
Mon-Thurs 9.30am – 5.30pm, Fri 9.30am – 2pm, Sun 9.30am – 1.30pm
**Services**
Mail order

Serving the local community with books and gifts of a Jewish nature.

## Catholic Truth Society Bookshop

**Address**   25a Ashley Place
London
SW1P 1LT
**Tel**   020 7821 1363
**Fax**   020 7821 7398
**Opening hours**
Mon-Fri 9.30am – 5.30pm, Sat 10am – 2pm

Dedicated to serious theology and books for the Catholic faith as well as providing a range of church requisites and cards.

## CCBI Bookroom

**Address**   Inter-Church House
35-41 Lower Marsh
London
SE1 7RL
**Tel**   020 7620 4444
**Fax**   020 7928 0010
**Opening hours**
Mon-Fri 9am – 4pm

Christian books, tapes and videos.

## Centre for Peace

**Address**   Cardinal Heenan Centre
326 High Road
Ilford
Essex
IG1 1QP
**Tel**   020 8478 3068
**Opening hours**
Mon-Sat 9.45am – 5pm

Range of books on theology and related subjects located in the Cardinal Heenan Centre.

## Chapter and Verse

**Address**   32 Fife Road
Kingston upon Thames
Surrey
KT1 1SO
**Tel/Fax**   020 8547 2617
**Web**
www.chapterandverse.co.uk
**Email**
info@chapterandverse.co.uk
**Opening hours**
Mon-Fri 9.30am – 6pm (Thurs 9.30am – 7pm), Sat 9am – 6pm

General Christian bookshop.

## Chapter Two

**Address**   199 Plumstead Common
Road
Plumpstead Common
London
SE18 2UJ
**Tel**   020 8316 4972
**Fax**   020 8854 5963
**Email**
Ecross7023@aol.com
**Opening hours**
Mon-Fri 9.30am – 5.30pm (lunch 1pm – 2.30pm), Sat 10.30am – 1pm
**Services**
Mail order, catalogues

Originally a bookstall in Woolwich Market and now a registered charity with a shop. The bookshop is run by volunteers and trustees and their aim is to promote Christian knowledge worldwide. The Plymouth Brethren and dispensational theology are the main themes. Customers travelling from a distance are advised to ring ahead so they can put the kettle on ready for your arrival.

## Christian Book Centre

**Address**   London Bible College
Green Lane
Northwood
Middlesex
HA6 2UW
**Tel**   01923 826061, ext. 201
**Fax**   01923 836530
**Web**
www.londonbiblecollege.ac.uk
**Email**
mailbox@londonbiblecollege.ac.uk
**Opening hours**
Mon-Fri 9.30am – 4.45pm

## Christian Books and Music

**Address**   Kensington Temple
Kensington Park Road
London
W11
**Tel**   020 7727 8684
**Opening hours**
Tues-Fri 10am – 7pm, Sat 10am – 6pm

## Christian Bookshop

**Address**   275 Ewell Road
Surbiton
Surrey
KT6
**Tel**   020 8399 8363
**Opening hours**
Tues 10am – 5.30pm, Wed-Fri 9am –
5.30pm, Sat 9am – 4pm

## Christian City Books

**Address**   76 Bolton Crescent
London
SE5 0SE
**Tel/Fax**   020 7582 1299
**Email**

dunamis@compuserve.com
**Opening hours**
Tues, Wed, Fri 10am – 6pm, Thurs
10am – 7pm, Sat 11am – 3pm

Started by Youth With A Mission
and ready to save you money as
well as save your soul with 10%
discount on all bibles.

## Christian Literature Crusade

**Branch**   Morley House
26-30 Holborn Viaduct
London
EC1 2AQ
**Tel**   020 7583 4835/ 4837
**Fax**   020 7583 6059
**Email**
clcuklond@aol.com
**Opening hours**
Mon-Fri 10am – 5.30pm (Thurs 10am
– 6pm), Sat 10am  – 5pm

**Branch**   13 Upper Wickham Lane
Welling
DA16 3AA
**Tel**   020 8301 4641
**Opening hours**
Mon-Sat 9.30am – 5.30pm

The central London shop consists of
two floors dedicated to books and
music of evangelical and charis-
matic Christian literature. There is
also a good selection of books in
foreign languages.

## Church House Bookshop

**Address**   31 Great Smith Street
Westminster
London
SW1P 3BN

**Tel** 020 7340 0280
**Fax** 020 7340 0278
**Web**
www.chbookshop.co.uk
**Email**
Bookshop@c-of-e.org.uk
**Opening hours**
Mon-Fri 9am – 5pm
**Services**
Mail order, signings, catalogues, events

The official Church of England bookshop and outlet for Church House Publications is a short walk from Westminster Abbey. They sell all the usual literature related to Christianity and were voted Christian Bookseller of the Year in 1998.

## Comparative Religion Centre

**Address** 359 Rayners Lane
Pinner
Middlesex
HA5 5EN
**Tel** 020 8426 2216
**Fax** 020 8426 2217
**Web**
www.wipecrc.com
**Email**
info@wipecrc.com
**Opening hours**
Mon-Sat 10am – 6pm
**Services**
Mail order, catalogues

Registered with the local council as an official resource centre for Islam. They have a range of books, videos and multimedia on all aspects of Islam as well as holding lectures and seminars.

## Cornerstone

**Address** Christian Bookshop
45-51 Woodhouse Road
North Finchley
London
N12 0NL
**Tel** 020 8446 3056
**Fax** 020 8446 2227
**Email**
cs@cornerstone4551.freeserve.co.uk
**Opening hours**
Mon-Sat 9.30am – 5.30pm
**Services**
Mail order, catalogues

Established as a resource centre for local churches and to promote the Christian faith through the sale of books and other related items.

## Dar Al-Taqwa

**Address** 7a Melcombe Street
London
NW1 6AE
**Tel** 020 7935 6385
**Fax** 020 7224 3894
**Opening hours**
Mon-Sat 9am – 6pm

Religious books on the Islamic faith and the Middle East in Arabic and English. Language learning books, dictionaries and children's books feature too along with crafts and music.

## Daybreak Books

**Address** 68 Baring Road
Lee
London
SE12 0PS
**Tel** 020 8690 2790
**Opening hours**
Tues-Fri 9am – 5.30pm, Sat 9am – 5pm

**Services**
Mail order

Founded over 20 years ago by the South Lee Christian Centre, they provide the local area with a whole range of Christian literature.

## Dovecote Christian Bookshop

**Address**    22 South Street
                Epsom
                Surrey
                KT18 7PF
**Tel**          01372 817707
**Opening hours**
Mon-Sat 10am – 5pm
**Services**
Mail order, events

Founded in 1996, this all dominations Christian bookshop is located in one of the oldest buildings in Epsom Town Square. It has a coffee shop within and also stocks music as well as the usual fare of bibles and Christian literature.

## Emel Books

**Address**    5-6 Star Mews
                52a Windus Road
                London
                N16 6UP
**Tel**          020 8806 9970
**Fax**          020 8806 9848
**Opening hours**
By appointment
**Services**
Book lists

Highly specialised outlet dealing in literature concerned with Hebraica and Judaica. Visits are by appointment only.

## Faith House Bookshop

**Address**    7 Tufton Street
                London
                SE19 2SB
**Tel**          020 7222 6952
**Fax**          020 7976 7180
**Opening hours**
Mon-Fri 9am – 5pm (Thurs 9am – 6pm)
**Services**
Mail order, catalogues, events, signings

Located behind Westminster Abbey, this is the official bookshop of the Church Union. Aside from the usual range of bibles and religious texts you will find a large range of religious icons, rosaries and crucifixes.

## Good News Christian

**Address**    50 Churchfield Road
                Acton
                London
                W3 6DL
**Tel**          020 8992 7123
**Opening hours**
Mon-Sat 9am – 5.30pm (Thurs 9am – 7pm)

## Havering Christian Bookshop

**Address**    80 Victoria Road
                Romford
                Essex
                RM1 2LT
**Tel**          01708 727625
**Opening hours**
Mon-Sat 9.30am – 5.30pm

Books, music, videos and gifts with a Christian theme.

## Hebrew Books & Gifts

**Address**  24 Amhurst Parade
Amhurst Park
London
N16 5AA
**Tel**  020 8802 0609
**Fax**  020 8802 4567
**Opening hours**
Mon-Thurs 9.30am – 7.30pm, Sun, Fri
9.30am – 2.30pm
**Services**
Mail order, catalogues

Specialising in Hebrew and English
books based around the Bible and
the Talmud. All aspects of Jewish
history and culture are covered
here.

## Holy Cross Catholic Bookshop

**Address**  4 Brownhill Road
London
SE6
**Tel**  020 8461 0896
**Opening hours**
Tues-Sat 11am – 5pm

## Islamic Book Centre

**Address**  120 Drummond Street
London
NW1 2HL
**Tel**  020 7388 0710
**Opening hours**
Mon-Sat 9.30am – 6pm

Books in English, Arabic and other
languages of the Muslim world
covering a wide range of topics
related to the Middle East and its
religions.

## Jambala Bookshop

**Address**  247 Globe Road
Bethnal Green
London
E2 0JD
**Tel**  020 8981 4037
**Opening hours**
Mon-Sat 10.30am – 5.30pm

Part of a Buddhist village – the
London Buddhist Centre is close by
– they sell mainly books to do with
the Buddhist faith alongside some
children's titles and fiction. New age
titles are also included in an eclectic
mix that contributes to a welcoming
and interesting bookshop. The
Cherry Orchard vegetarian restaurant is located next door and that
alone is a reason to visit this part of
London.

## Jerusalem the Golden

**Address**  146-148 Golders Green Road
Golders Green
London
NW11 8HE
**Tel**  020 8455 4960
**Opening hours**
Mon, Weds 9.30am – 6pm, Tues,
Thurs, Sun 9.30am – 10pm, Fri 9.30am
– 4.30pm in summer (to 1.30pm in
winter)

One room is devoted to books for
children and the other to adults.
They claim to have the largest selection of Hebrew music and videos in
Europe, along with a wide choice of
bibles, references and books on
religious education.

## Jewish Memorial Council Bookshop

**Address**   25-26 Enford Street
London
W1H 2DD
**Tel**   020 7724 7778
**Fax**   020 7706 1710
**Email**
jmcbooks@btinternet.com
**Opening hours**
Mon-Thurs 9.30am – 5.30pm, Fri
9.30am – 4pm, Sun 10.30am – 2pm
**Services**
Mail order, catalogues

Serving the Jewish community for over 70 years, the Council and its bookshop stocks books in English and Yiddish, covering the whole range of the Jewish world. They also sell religious service and Jewish holiday texts as well as Hebrew dictionaries, books for children and travel books on Israel.

## John Thornton

**Address**   455 Fulham Road
London
SW10 9UZ
**Tel**   020 7352 8810

The number of titles in stock is around 10,000, a large portion of which is theology. They are mostly secondhand but they also specialise in rare and antiquarian books with prices ranging from 50p to £500.

## King and I Christian Shop

**Address**   241 Graham Road
London
E8

**Tel**   020 8525 5600
**Opening hours**
Mon-Wed 10am – 5.30pm, Thurs-Sat
10am – 6.30pm

## London Buddhist Centre

**Address**   51 Roman Road
London
E2 0HU
**Tel**   020 8981 1225
**Opening hours**
Mon-Fri 10am – 5pm

Primarily a centre for training courses and classes. A sister location to the nearby Jambala Bookshop, there is a good stock of Buddhist works in English translation along with other associated products such as incense, candles, meditation cushions and such like.

## London City Mission

**Address**   175 Tower Bridge Road
London
SE1 2AH
**Tel**   020 7407 7585
**Fax**   020 7403 6711
**Web**
www.icm.org.uk
**Email**
icm.uk@btinternet.com
**Opening hours**
Mon-Fri 9am – 4.30pm

Set up by David Naismith in 1835 with the aim of bringing the Christian gospel to those who are outside the influence of the church. The aim is as strong today as ever. The bookshop is on the first floor.

## Manor House Books

**Address**   80 East End Road
Finchley
London
N3 2SY
**Tel**   020 8349 9484
**Fax**   020 8346 7430
**Web**
www.bibliophile.net/John-Trotter-Books.htm
**Email**
MHB@jt96.demon.co.uk
**Opening hours**
Mon-Thurs 10am – 5pm, Sun 10am –
1pm
**Services**
Mail order, catalogues

One of the largest stocks of rare,
secondhand and new books on
Judaism in Europe, covering children's Jewish books, the Middle
East, Holocaust studies, Hebrew,
Yiddish and a selection of bargain
books. They will also provide a
printout of all Jewish books in print
for a nominal charge.

## Marantha Christian Bookshop

**Address**   22 Windsor Street
Uxbridge
Middlesex
UB8 1AB
**Tel**   01895 255748
**Fax**   01895 811383
**Web**
www.maranthabookshop.co.uk
**Email**
geoff@maranthabookshop.co.uk
**Opening hours**
Mon-Sat 9am – 5.30pm (Thurs 9am –
7pm)

**Services**
Mail order, catalogues, events

Located in the oldest street in
Uxbridge.

## Masters Christian Books

**Address**   19 Goodmayes Road
Goodmayes
Ilford
Essex
1G3 4UH
**Tel**   020 8598 8411
**Fax**   020 8599 3356
**Opening hours**
Mon-Sat 10am – 5.30pm (Thurs 1pm –
5pm)

Run by a husband-and-wife team,
their aim is to provide Christian
support to the local community.
Alongside the usual array of
Christian literature they also offer
counselling and prayer services.

## Menorah Print and Gift Centre

**Address**   16 Russell Parade
Golders Green
London
NW11 9NN
**Tel**   020 8458 8289
**Opening hours**
Sun-Thurs 9.30am – 6pm, Fri 9.30am –
2pm

Deals extensively with literature on
Judaica and Judaism, with a small
selection of religious items appropriate to Jewish holidays and
festivals.

## Mesoiroh Seforim Bookshop

**Address**    61 Oldhill Street
London
N16 6LU
**Tel**    020 8809 4310
**Opening hours**
Mon-Sun 9am – 9.30pm (Fri until 4pm in summer and until 1pm in winter)

Mainly a specialist publisher of books in Hebrew but also stocks a selected range of educational and children's titles in English and Hebrew. Yiddish is the speciality though.

## Methodist Church Bookshop

**Address**    25 Marylebone Road
London
NW1 5JR
**Tel**    020 7486 5502
**Fax**    020 7935 1507
**Email**
bookshop@methodistchurch.org.uk
**Opening hours**
Mon-Fri 10am – 4pm
**Services**
Mail order, catalogues

Housed on the lower ground floor of Methodist Church House, the bookshop was formed in the 1930s to supply overseas missionaries with books. Today they still supply Methodist and theological publications worldwide. Stocks new books on religion and theology plus some music, cards and stationery.

## Mowbray's

**Address**    Waterstone's
28 Margaret Street
London
W1N
**Tel**    020 7436 0294
**Opening hours**
Mon-Fri 9am – 6pm (Thurs 9am – 7pm), Sat 9.30am – 6pm
**Services**
Mail order

Mowbray's was once considered to be one of the most interesting general bookshops in London but it is for its long history as a specialist religious outlet that it is best known today. Bought and refurbished by Dillons in the late '80s, it re-established itself as one of the best religious booksellers in the capital. There are few places that can compete with this depth of stock and expertise. Of particular note is the range of church requisites available: candles, devotional objects and genuine palm crosses at Easter. It is also a general bookshop with the usual range across the main subject areas for this size of chain bookstore.

## Muslim Bookshop

**Address**    233 Seven Sisters Road
London
N4 2DA
**Tel**    020 7272 3214
**Opening hours**
Mon-Sun 10am – 9pm

Books on Islam and related topics, in Arabic and English. Also a range of associated products from maps to clothing.

## Mustard Seed

**Address**   21 Kentish Town Road
London
NW1 8NT
**Tel**   020 7267 5646
**Opening hours**
Mon-Fri 12.30pm – 7pm

This bookshop specialises in the Creation debate. Christian apologetics are at home here with a wide selection of books and tapes on this major issue, just one minute's walk from Camden Town tube station

## Padre Pio Bookshop

**Address**   264 Vauxhall Bridge Road
London
SW1V 1BB
**Tel**   020 7834 5363
**Opening hours**
Mon-Fri 10am – 5.30pm

Dedicated to Padre Pio, the stigmatised monk. There is a large range of Roman Catholic publications, particularly on devotional teaching.

## Pendlebury's Bookshop

**Address**   Church House
Portland Avenue
Stamford Hill
London
N16 6HJ
**Tel/Fax**   020 8809 4922
**Web**
www.clique.co.uk/pendleburys
**Email**
books@pendleburys.demon.co.uk
**Opening hours**
Mon-Sat 10am – 5pm
**Services**

Mail order, catalogues

Tucked away in a disused church in the north London area of Stamford Hill, Pendlebury's has been here since 1984 and boasts the largest secondhand and antiquarian stock of theological books in the country.

## Protestant Truth Society

**Address**   184 Fleet Street
London
EC4A 2HJ
**Tel**   020 7405 4960
**Opening hours**
Mon-Fri 9am – 5.30pm

The society was founded in 1889 and has been in Fleet Street since 1947. This bookshop stocks primarily Protestant reformed and evangelical literature, greetings cards and social stationery.

## Quaker Bookshop

**Address**   Friends House
173-177 Euston Road
London
NW1 2BJ
**Tel**   020 7663 1030
**Fax**   020 7663 1001
**Web**
www.quaker.org.uk
**Email**
bookshop@quaker.org.uk
**Opening hours**
Tues-Fri 10am – 5pm
**Services**
Mail order, catalogues

Housed in Friends House, the administrative centre for the Quaker religion. The building houses a café and art gallery as well as the bookshop. The range of new and secondhand stock concentrates on pacifism, liberal Christianity and world religions.

## Russian Orthodox Cathedral Bookshop

**Address**  67 Ennismore Gardens
London
SW7 1NH
**Tel**  020 7584 0096
**Opening hours**
Only after services and on Sunday until 1pm

Located inside the Cathedral of the Assumption and All Saints and strictly for followers of Orthodox Christianity.

## SPCK Bookshop

**Branch**  Holy Trinity Church
Marylebone Road
London
NW1 4DU
**Tel**  020 7388 1659
**Fax**  020 7388 2352
**Web**
www.spck.org.uk
**Email**
london@spck.org.uk
**Opening hours**
Mon-Fri 9am – 5pm

**Branch**  Partnership House
157 Waterloo Road
London
SE1 8XA
**Tel/Fax**  020 7633 9096
**Web**  www.spck.org.uk
**Email**  partnership@spck.org.uk
**Opening hours**
Mon-Fri 10.30am – 4.30pm

The SPCK (Society for Promoting of Christian Knowledge) specialises in religion and theology: bibles, sermons, doctrines, spirituality and all associated subjects. In addition to the general Christian books they stock selection of bargain books, music, candles, cards and a full range of church requisites.

**Branch**  Secondhand & Antiquarian
Holy Trinity Church
Marylebone Road
London
NW1 4DU
**Tel**  020 7383 3097
**Fax**  020 7388 2352
**Email**
secondhand@spck.org.uk
**Opening hours**
Mon-Sat 9.30am – 6pm
**Services**
Mail order

The second shop at this location is found right at the back of the church. Formerly Charles Higham, a secondhand and antiquarian specialist of repute, it is now under the banner of SPCK, dealing in secondhand and antiquarian books on theology, church architecture, history, music and literature.

## Spurgeons Book Room

**Address**  189 South Norwood Hill
Norwood
London
SE25 6DJ
**Tel/Fax**  020 8653 3640
**Opening hours**
Mon-Fri 10am – 4pm

Mainly a college-run service devoted to theology and religion.

## St Martin-in-the-Field

**Address**  The Crypt
Trafalgar Square
London
WC2N 4JJ
**Tel**  020 7839 8362
**Opening hours**
Mon-Sat 10am – 6pm, Sun noon – 6pm

The entrance is off Duncannon Street, to the south of the church and on the east side of Trafalgar Square. Go down the steps and you will find the shop next to the café and the London Brass Rubbing Centre. There is a small and there-fore shallow selection of books on religion and theology. Above ground there are market stalls selling books but usually anything interesting has long been spotted by eagle-eyed dealers.

## St Paul Multimedia

**Address**  199 Kensington High Street
London
W8 6BA
**Tel**  020 7937 9591
**Fax**  020 7937 9910
**Email**
london@stpaulmultimedia.co.uk
**Opening hours**
Mon-Sat 9.30am – 5.30pm

Books covering the whole range of Christian literature with an exten-sive range of music and videos.

## St Paul's

**Address**  Morpeth Terrace
Victoria
London
SW1P 1EP
**Tel**  020 7828 5582
**Fax**  020 7828 3329
**Email**
bookshop@stpauls.org.uk
**Opening hours**
Mon-Sat 9.30am – 6pm
**Services**
Mail order, events, signings

Owned and managed by the Society of St Paul, it was formerly the Westminster Cathedral Bookshop. Although the name has changed it is still part of the Cathedral just 200 metres from Victoria station. They are focused on the Catholic faith with a wide range of books and multimedia products in a nicely laid out and well-organised shop.

## Swedenborg Society Bookshop

**Address**  20-21 Bloomsbury Way
London
WC1A 2TH
**Tel**  020 7405 7986
**Opening hours**
Mon-Fri 9.30am – 5pm

The Swedenborg Society was founded in 1810 in honour of the Swedish scientist and theologian whose mystical ideas became the basis of a religious movement. For the last 70 years Swedenborg's writings, related books and biogra-phies have been sold from this listed building. There is also a reference and lending library on the premises.

## Tibet Shop

**Address** 10 Bloomsbury Way
London
WC1A 2SH
**Tel** 020 7405 5284
**Fax** 020 7404 2336

*See Countries*

## Wesley Owen

**Branch** 82 High Road
South Woodford
London
E18
**Tel** 020 8530 4244

**Branch** 16 Park Street
Croydon
Surrey
CR0 1YE
**Tel** 020 8686 2772

**Branch** 111 Cecil Road
Enfield
Middlesex
EN2
**Tel** 020 8363 8517

**Branch** 21 The Mall
Bromley
Kent
BR1 1TR
**Tel** 020 8464 1191

**Branch** 14 Bond Street
Ealing
London
W5
**Tel** 020 8579 9242

**Branch** 11 Mason Avenue
Wealdstone
Harrow

Middlesex
HA3
**Tel** 020 8861 3259

**Branch** 3 Eccleston Street
London
SW1W
**Tel** 020 7463 1451

**Branch** 3-9 Wigmore Street
London
W1H 0AD
**Tel** 020 7493 1851
**Fax** 020 7493 4478
**Opening hours**
Mon-Fri 9.30am – 6pm, Sat 9.30am –
5.30pm

**Branch** 14 Eton Street
Richmond
Surrey
TW9
**Tel** 020 8940 2915

**Branch** 5 Grove Road
Sutton
Surrey
**Tel** 020 8642 6511

Wesley Owen is a nationwide chain specialising in Christian books and music with a number of branches in and around London, all listed here. The opening hours for all of the London shops are Mon-Fri 9am – 5.30pm with the exception of their largest shop at Wigmore Street W1, which is open until 6pm Mon-Fri. They also have a web site at www.wesleyowen.com

## Wisdom Books

**Address**   402 Hoe Street
                        London
                        E17 9AA
**Tel**          020 8520 5588
**Opening hours**
Mon-Fri 9.30am – 5.30pm, Sat
10.30am – 4.30pm

Wisdom books is primarily a mail
order and book distribution operation. Wisdom Publications was
founded in 1978 under the spiritual
guidance of two Tibetan Lamas
whose purpose was to keep Tibetan
Buddhism alive during the oppres-
sive Chinese occupation of Tibet
and to promote Buddhism in the
West. You have to ring the doorbell
to be admitted to the first-floor
bookshop and once inside you can
select from one of the most comprehensive collections in London of
books on Buddhism.

# Notes

# *Secondhand*

## Abbey Bookshop

**Address**   1d Market Hall
Camden Lock
Chalk Farm Road
London
NW1 8AT
**Tel**   020 7424 9110
**Opening hours**
Mon-Fri 9.30am – 6pm, Sat, Sun
9.30am – 6.30pm

A good selection of secondhand
books can be found at this popular
little shop. Subjects are varied and
prices are good.

## Alexandra Bookshop

**Address**   209 Park Road
London
N8 8JG
**Tel**   020 8889 1674
**Opening hours**
Thurs-Sat 10am – 5.30pm

Appropriately called the Alexandra
Bookshop due to its position near
the Palace but the fascia reads
'Skywalkers'. Nevertheless, sandwiched as it is between a pub and
estate agents there is always something appealing in the window of
this little bookshop and the stock
seems to tick over nicely.

## Alison Knox Bookseller

**Address**   53 Exmouth Market
London
EC1R 4QL
**Tel**   020 7833 0591

**Opening hours**
Mon-Sat 10.30am – 5.30pm
**Services**
Mail order, catalogues

A shop which deals mainly in art, architecture, reference books and angling. The fishing side is represented by a regular catalogue.

## Any Amount of Books

**Address**   62 Charing Cross Road
London
WC2H 0BB
**Tel**   020 7240 8140
**Fax**   020 7240 1769
**Web**
www.anyamountofbooks.com
**Email**
charingx@anyamountofbooks.com
**Opening hours**
Mon-Sat 10.30am – 9.30pm, Sun
10.30am – 7.30pm

Secondhand books thoroughly weeded of any potential discoveries by the hordes of browsers who patrol London's main book thoroughfare. Along with many first editions there are plenty of cheap books and leather by the yard for those who need it.

## Archive Bookstore

**Address**   83 Bell Street
London
NW1 6TB
**Tel**   020 7402 8212
**Opening hours**
Mon-Sat 10.30am – 6pm

Books spill on to the street at this jumbled bookstore. All types of books are found here but they have

a particular leaning towards music.

## Bargain Books

**Address**   3 Market Square
Uxbridge
Middlesex
UB8 1LH
**Tel**   01895 257646
**Opening hours**
Mon-Sat 9am – 5pm

Devoted entirely to fiction and particularly the Mills and Boon romance range.

## H Baron

**Address**   76 Fortune Green Road
London
NW6
**Tel**   020 7794 4041
**Opening hours**
Fri-Sat 1pm – 6pm

*See Performing Arts*

## Benedicts Bookshop

**Address**   92 Lillie Road
London
SW16 7SR
**Tel**   020 7385 4426
**Opening hours**
Mon-Sat 10am – 6pm

A small stock of new and secondhand books is available from this friendly little bookshop.

## Blackheath Bookshop

**Address**   74 Tranquil Vale
Blackheath
London
SE3
**Tel**   020 8852 4786

**Opening hours**
Mon-Sat 9am – 5pm

A comprehensive stock of second-hand books, although there are some new paperbacks too. Local history is well represented, as is travel, military and maritime. You may also find some modern first editions in this bookshop made for browsing.

## Bloomsbury Bookshop

**Address** 12 Bury Place
London
WC1A 2JL
**Tel** 020 7404 7433

*See Literature*

## Book Exchange

**Address** 120 Shenley Road
Borehamwood
WD6
**Tel** 020 8236 0966
**Fax** 020 8953 6673
**Email**
dee4bee@compuserve.com
**Opening hours**
Mon-Sat 9.30am – 5.30pm

Providing Borehamwood with a good range of secondhand books, they particularly favour history, travel and military. Some new paperback fiction and bargain books are also on offer.

## Bookmongers

**Address** 439 Coldharbour Lane
Brixton
London
SW9 8LN
**Tel** 020 7738 4225

**Opening hours**
Mon-Sat 10.30am – 6.30pm

A great place to rummage and browse amongst a wide range of general secondhand books with prices as low as 50p.

## Books and Bits

**Address** 28 Brockley Cross
London
SE4
**Tel** 020 8692 9480
**Opening hours**
Mon-Sat 9.30am – 5.30pm

An average range of secondhand books somewhat curiously alongside a selection of glass and chinaware.

## Books and Bygones

**Address** 52 Hayes Street
Hayes Village
Bromley
Kent
BR2
**Tel** 020 8462 3550
**Opening hours**
Mon-Sat 9am – 5.30pm
**Services**
Mail order, catalogues

The owner of this general second-hand bookshop has an interest in modern first editions so a visit may reveal something of interest.

## Books Bookshop

**Address** 53 West Ham Lane
Stratford
London
E15 4PH
**Tel** 020 8534 8455

**Opening hours**
Mon-Fri 10am – 6pm, Sat 10am – 5pm

Founded in 1995 as a general secondhand bookshop, this is uniquely home to an estate agent and martial arts group, which explains the kickbag hanging in the middle of the shop. It is a great place to browse with a wide variety of books on all sorts of subjects. You'll find everything from rare finds to utter rubbish.

## Books Bought and Sold

**Address**   68 Walton Road
              East Molesey
              Surrey
              KT8 0DL
**Tel**       020 8224 3232
**Fax**       020 8224 3576
**Opening hours**
Tues-Sat 10am – 5pm

*See Transport & Military*

## Books for Amnesty International

**Address**   139b King Street
              Hammersmith
              London
              W6 9JG
**Tel**       020 8746 3172
**Opening hours**
Mon-Fri 10am – 6pm, Sat 10am – 4pm

Plenty of secondhand books across a wide range of subject areas for the good cause of Amnesty International. They are reliant on donations for stock so please bring your unwanted books here. The shop also serves as a meeting place and information centre.

## Charing Cross Road Bookshop

**Address**   56 Charing Cross Road
              London
              WC2H 0BB
**Tel**       020 7836 3697
**Fax**       020 740 1769
**Opening hours**
Mon-Sat 10.30am – 9.30pm, Sun 10.30am – 7.30pm

One of the scruffiest bookshops in London but with a prodigious turnover of stock over a wide range of general subjects.

## Church Street Bookshop

**Address**   142 Church Street
              Stoke Newington
              London
              N16 0JU
**Tel**       020 7241 5411
**Opening hours**
Mon-Sun 11.30am – 6pm

One of many bookshops in this popular area of London. Academic paperbacks dominate, particularly history, although they do have a more general range.

## Coffeehouse Bookshop

**Address**   139 Greenwich South Street
              Greenwich
              London
              SE1D 8NX
**Tel**       020 8692 3885
**Opening hours**

Mon-Sat 10am – 5.30pm, Sun 11.30am – 5.30pm

Secondhand books, tapes, records, CDs, videos, sheet music and other bric-a-brac are sold here and have been for over 20 years.

## Crouch End Bookshop

**Address**   12 Park Road
Crouch End
London
N8 8AG
**Tel**   020 8348 8966
**Opening hours**
Tues, Wed, Sat 10am – 6pm, Thurs, Fri 10am – 7pm, Sun noon – 7pm

Small secondhand bookshop in Crouch End with a reasonable range of books, particularly paperbacks.

## Croydon Bookshop

**Address**   304 Carshalton Road
Carshalton
SM3 3QB
**Tel**   020 8643 6857
**Opening hours**
Tues-Sat 10.30am – 5.30pm

Mainly secondhand but with a few antiquarian books.

## Crusaid

**Address**   17-19 Upper Tachbrook Street
London
SW1P 1JU
**Tel**   020 7233 8736
**Opening hours**
Mon-Sat 10.30am – 5.15pm (Tues 11.30am – 5.15pm)

A good selection of books with the added advantage of knowing your purchases benefit a charity.

## Dartford Books

**Address**   7a Spital Street
Dartford
Kent
DA1 2DJ
**Tel**   01322 222606
**Opening hours**
Mon-Sat 9am – 5pm

Anything and everything can be found in this well-established shop with over ten years' experience.

## Earlsfield Bookshop

**Address**   513 Garrat Lane
Wandsworth
London
SW18 4SW
**Tel**   020 7946 3744
**Opening hours**
Mon-Thurs 4pm – 6pm, Sat 10am – 5pm

Nestled next to Earslfield station, this quaint-looking bookshop is only open for two hours a day during the week but it will be two hours well spent if you do make a visit to browse the general secondhand stock on offer.

## Edward Terry Bookseller

**Address**   26 Chapel Road
Ilford
Essex
IG1 2HG
**Tel**   020 8478 2850
**Opening hours**
Mon-Fri 9.30am – 5.30pm

Secondhand and bargain books galore on all subjects.

## Enigma Books

**Address**   16 Church Road
Crystal Palace
London
SE19 2ET
**Tel**   020 8653 1884
**Opening hours**
Mon-Sat 10am – 6pm, Sun 11am – 5pm

A new addition to the bookselling fraternity offers a general range of secondhand books and records with plenty of choice for under £5.

## Exchange Books

**Address**   792 Holloway Road
London
N19
**Tel**   020 7281 7382
**Opening hours**
Mon-Sat 11am – 9pm

General range of secondhand books, especially paperbacks, covering most popular subjects with some new titles thrown in for good measure.

## For Books

**Address**   58 Cowcross Street
London
EC1M 6BP
**Tel**   020 7336 6533
**Opening hours**
Mon-Fri 8am – 8pm, Sat 10am – 6pm

A veritable feast of secondhand books and plenty of new books at bargain prices are to be found at this location opposite Farringdon

station. They have a broad range including fiction, crime, travel and academic titles too.

## Fortune Green Bookshop

**Address**   74 Fortune Green Road
London
NW6 1DS
**Tel**   020 7435 7545
**Fax**   020 7794 4937
**Email**
belleric@dircon.co.uk
**Opening hours**
Wed-Sat 10.30am – 5.30pm
**Services**
Mail order, catalogues

Secondhand, antiquarian and remainder books is the order of the day in this west Hampstead book-shop. They have a strong leaning towards women's writers and books on women's history and their regular catalogues of 19th- and early 20th-century literature are also a feature of this pleasant shop.

## WA Foster

**Address**   183 Chiswick High Road
London
W4 2DR
**Tel**   020 8995 2768
**Opening hours**
Mon-Sat 10.30am – 6pm

An attractive shop that claims to be the oldest in Chiswick. It has been providing secondhand and anti-quarian books to local book buyers for over 20 years. One thing that still stands out about this bookshop is that only books in very good to fine condition are stocked. As a result, the sections of art and illustrated books and fine bindings are particularly good.

## Glasheens Bookshop

**Address**  5 Burwood Parade
Guildford Street
Chertsey
Surrey
KT16 9AE
**Tel**  01932 562555
**Opening hours**
Mon-Sat 9.30am – 5pm
**Services**
Mail order

A small family-run concern in the heart of Chertsey's main shopping area. They offer mainly secondhand books on most subjects as well as a small section for new books.

## Gloucester Road Bookshop

**Address**  123 Gloucester Road
London
SW7 4TE
**Tel**  020 7370 3503
**Fax**  020 7373 0610
**Opening hours**
Mon-Fri 8.30am – 10.30pm, Sat, Sun
10.30am – 6.30pm
**Services**
Catalogues

An adventurous secondhand bookshop of some 15 years' standing. It is clearly a cut above the norm with long opening hours and a real desire to sell good-value books and please customers (a basic enough aim in retailing but not always evident in many secondhand bookshops). The

stock covers all the popular general areas with the arts, history and fiction sections standing out. Prints and postcards are also sold.

## Griffiths and Partners

**Address**  31-35 Great Ormond Street
London
WC1N 3HZ
**Tel**  020 7430 1394
**Opening hours**
Mon-Fri noon – 6pm, other times by appointment
**Services**
Mail order

Possibly the smallest bookshop in London, it is not surprisngly packed from floor to ceiling with books, covering every available inch of space in the shop and spilling out on to the street. The emphasis is on literature, especially poetry, travel (mainly the Middle East) and typography. A small range of bargain fiction titles is displayed outside.

## Halcyon Books

**Branch**  1 Greenwich South Street
Greenwich
London
SE10 8NW
**Tel**  020 8305 2675
**Opening hours**
Mon-Sun 10am – 6pm
**Services**
Mail order

**Branch**  22 Nelson Road
Greenwich
London
SE10 9JB
**Tel**  020 8853 0674

**Opening hours**
Mon-Sun 10am – 6pm

Great range of secondhand and bargain books covering all the main subject areas.

# Handsworth Books

**Address**  148 Charing Cross Road
London
WC2H 0LB
**Tel**  020 7240 3566
**Web**
www.abebooks.com/home/handsworth
**Email**
steve@handsworthbooks.demon.co.uk
**Opening hours**
Mon-Sat 10.30am – 7.30pm, Sun noon – 6pm

Hidden away in the basement of the bargain bookshop Bookcase 9 on Charing Cross Road, it is worth delving in to see what's on offer. They are particularly strong on history and children's books at reasonable prices. They also have some remainders of relatively new fiction nicely priced at only 99p.

# Hayes Bookshop

**Address**  6 Glebe Avenue
Ickenham
Middlesex
UB10 8PB
**Tel**  01895 637725
**Opening hours**
Tues-Sat 10am – 5.30pm

A traditional secondhand bookshop supplying the local area since 1945.

# Henry Pordes

**Address**  58-60 Charing Cross Road
London
WC2H 0BB
**Tel**  020 7836 9031
**Fax**  020 7886 2201
**Opening hours**
Mon-Sat 10am – 7pm

Cellophane-covered books line the windows and indicate that the stock of literature and art is better than that on show in immediate second-hand shops. The rest is a mixture of general secondhand, some antiquarian and many remainders trying to look like bargains.

# Ian Sheridan Bookshop

**Address**  34 Thames Street
Hampton-On-Thames
Surrey
TW12 2DX
**Tel**  020 8979 1704
**Opening hours**
Mon-Sun 10.30am – 5pm

Packed full of piles of dusty volumes on the main road along the river.

# John Thornton

**Address**  455 Fulham Road
London
SW10 9UZ
**Tel**  020 7352 8810
**Opening hours**
Mon-Sat 10am – 5.30pm

*See Religion & Theology*

# Judd Two Books

**Address**  82 Marchmont Street
London

WC1N 1AG
**Tel** 020 7387 5333
**Opening hours**
Mon-Sat 11am – 7pm, Sun 11am – 6pm

A few minutes from Gay's the Word is this excellent bookshop packed to the ceiling with secondhand books of every description. Their buying-in of stock must be good as there is always something new and appealing for the many regular customers.

## Keith Fawkes

**Address** 1-3 Flask Walk
Hampstead
London, NW3 1HJ
**Tel** 020 7435 0614
**Opening hours**
Mon-Sat 10am – 5.30pm, Sun 1pm – 6pm

Three display windows beckon the browser and collector to this fascinating emporium of secondhand and antiquarian books. It can be a complete mess inside with piles of unsorted books getting in the way of casual browsing.

## Magpie Bookshop

**Branch** 53 Brushfield Street
Spitalfields
London, E1 6AA
**Tel** 020 7247 4263
**Opening hours**
Mon-Sat 11am – 6pm, Sun 10am – 6pm

**Branch** The Clerks House
118 Shoreditch High Street
London, E1
**Tel** 020 7729 5076

**Opening hours**
Mon-Sat 11am – 6pm

The Clerks House shop stands alone next to the church at the north end of Shoreditch High Street. Both branches are packed with books with an emphasis on science fiction paperbacks and comics from as little as 10p. There is also a good range of general topics such as history, film, cookery and crime.

## Marchmont Books

**Address** 39 Burton Street
London, WC1H 9AL
**Tel** 020 7387 7989
**Opening hours**
Mon-Fri 11am – 6.30pm

General secondhand books with an emphasis on literature and the arts. Some modern first editions, contemporary poetry and review copies.

## Marchpane

**Address** 16 Cecil Court
Charing Cross Road
London, WC2N 4HE
**Tel** 020 7836 8661
**Fax** 020 7497 0567
**Email**
kenneth@marchpane.demon.co.uk
**Opening hours**
Mon-Sat 10.30am – 6.30pm
**Services**
Catalogues

*See Children's*

## Martin Gladman

**Address** 235 Nether Street
Finchley

London
N3 1NT
**Tel** 020 8343 3023
**Opening hours**
Tues-Fri 11am – 8pm, Sat 10am – 6pm
**Services**
Mail order

A knowledgeable proprietor watches over this interesting little bookshop and his passion for books is matched only by his passion for stained-glass windows, in evidence above the door. There is a wide range of stock with a particular strength in social sciences and history. If you're lucky you may even be offered a cup of tea.

## Music and Video Exchange

**Branch** 480 Fulham Road
London, SW6
**Tel** 020 7385 5350
**Opening hours**
Mon-Sun 10am – 8pm

**Branch** 14 Pembridge Road
Notting Hill Gate
London
W11 3HT
**Tel** 020 7229 8420
**Opening hours**
Mon-Sun 10am – 8pm

A bookshop that bravely proclaims that it never refuses to buy books. The stock reflects this, in both condition and range. Inexpensive paperbacks predominate with a cheap selection of literary and genre fiction. Records and cassettes are also sold.

## My Back Pages

**Address** 8-10 Balham Station Road
London, SW12 9SG
**Tel** 020 8675 9346
**Opening hours**
Mon-Fri 10am – 8pm, Sat 10am – 6pm

Filled a gap in this part of London for a general secondhand bookshop, conveniently located 100 yards from Balham tube and railway stations. The hardback fiction section is good and it is possible to find the odd first edition at bargain prices, if not in the best condition. Paperbacks are in the majority and all general subjects are covered.

## Osterley Bookshop

**Address** 168a Thornbury Road
Osterley
Middlesex
TW7 4QE
**Tel** 020 8560 6206
**Email**
ostbks@email.infotrade.co.uk
**Opening hours**
Mon-Sun 10am – 5.30pm

An interesting location in the old Osterley and Spring Grove Piccadilly Line underground station and on the doorstep of Osterley Park. They have a good range of books from review stocks to antiquarian. There is always the possibility of stumbling across some hidden gem amongst this crammed shop.

## Paperback Exchange

**Address** 56 High Street
Sutton

Surrey
SM1 1EL
**Tel/Fax** 020 8770 1935
**Email**
pbx@sutton98.freeserve.co.uk
**Opening hours**
Mon-Sat 9.30am – 6pm
**Services**
Book search

Traditional paperback shop with an exchange system whereby they will credit the return of a book against your next purchase.

## Plus Books

**Address** 19 Abbey Parade
High Street
Merton
London
SW19
**Tel** 020 8542 1665
**Opening hours**
Mon-Sat 9.30am – 6pm

Paperbacks and magazines galore in this secondhand bookshop that has been selling and exchanging all types of fiction for over 30 years.

## Portobello Books

**Address** 328 Portobello Road
London
W10 5RU
**Tel** 020 8964 3166
**Opening hours**
Mon-Sat 10am – 6pm

Portobello Road has many things to offer, among them is this fine bookshop providing all who visit with a worthy selection of general secondhand books.

## Quinto

**Address** 48a Charing Cross Road
London
WC2H 0BB
**Tel** 020 7379 7669
**Fax** 020 7836 5977
**Opening hours**
Mon-Sat 9am – 9pm, Sun noon – 8pm

An interesting and varied collection of secondhand titles with a reasonable selection of modern firsts.

## Response Bookshop

**Address** 300 Old Brompton Road
London
SW5 9JF
**Tel** 020 7370 4606
**Fax** 020 7370 3918

*See Politics & Social Sciences*

## Richmond Bookshop

**Address** 20 Red Lion Street
Richmond
Surrey
TW9 1RW
**Tel** 020 8940 5512
**Opening hours**
Fri, Sat 9.30am – 6pm

A large but highly selective range of modern secondhand books, almost exclusively hardbacks. The opening hours are restrictive but do not deter the weekend regular who is determined to seek out quality secondhand books. Current review copies are always available and the illustrated art section stands out. The regular sales provide an opportunity to pick up a few bargains.

## Ripping Yarns

**Address**  355 Archway Road
London
N6 4EJ
**Tel**  020 8341 6111
**Fax**  020 7482 5056
**Web**
www.easyweb.easynet.co.uk/yarns
**Email**
yarns@easynet.co.uk
**Opening hours**
Mon-Fri 10.30am – 5.30pm, Sat 10am
– 5pm, Sun 11am – 4pm
**Services**
Catalogues

*See Children's*

## Robbie's Bookshop

**Address**  118a Alexandra Park Road
Muswell Hill
London
N10 2AE
**Tel**  020 8444 6957
**Opening hours**
Mon-Sat 9am – 5.30pm (closed Thurs)

A small, pleasant secondhand bookshop which has a general stock
range yet with an emphasis on
vintage and contemporary paperbacks.

## Skoob Books

**Address**  15 Sicilian Avenue
Southampton Row
London
WC1A 2QH
**Tel**  020 7404 3063
**Fax**  020 7404 4398
**Web**
www.skoob.com
**Email**

books@skoob.com
**Opening hours**
Mon-Sat 10.30am – 6.30pm
**Services**  Mail order

Skoobs is still renowned as one of
the best academic bookshops in the
capital and rightly so. They earned
their place at the top and have
maintained good standards through
strength in depth of stock, covering
literature, literary criticism, philosophy, history, art, music, social
sciences, business and economics.
The ethos is right, the execution
effective and the customers loyal
and satisfied. A bookish visitor or
student in London should not miss
a visit to Skoob.

## Skoob Two

**Address**  17 Sicilian Avenue
Southampton Row
London
WC1A
**Tel**  020 7405 0030
**Fax**  020 7404 4398
**Opening hours**
Mon-Sat 10.30am – 6.30pm

Added to the original Skoob in the
mid-'80s to cope with more books
than the original branch could
handle. Secondhand and antiquarian books with an academic theme
and esoteric bias along with science
and technology, classics, Oriental
studies and all religions are stocked
as adventurously as in the parent
shop.

## Spreadeagle Bookshop

**Address**   8 Nevada Street
              Greenwich
              London
              SE10 9JL
**Tel**        020 8305 1666
**Opening hours**
Mon-Sun 10am – 5.30pm

Located in an old coaching house and established as a bookshop in 1957. There are close to 20,000 antiquarian and secondhand books here with a good ranges on topography, history, performing arts, literature and maritime. The stock is very much non-technical and wants lists are welcomed.

## Stephen Foster

**Address**   95 Bell Street
              London
              NW1 6TL
**Tel/Fax**   020 7724 0876
**Opening hours**
Mon-Sat 10am – 6pm

*See Art & Design*

## Swans Bookshop

**Address**   5 Tooting Market
              Tooting High Street
              London
              SW17 0RH
**Tel**        020 8672 4980
**Opening hours**
Mon, Tue, Thurs 9am – 5pm, Fri, Sat 9am – 5.30pm

A real traditional secondhand London bookshop which has been on this site for almost 30 years. The business was originally started 80 years ago with a barrow in Deptford Market which was followed by a stall then a shop. The stock, although secondhand, is not as old as the business and there is always something of interest among the fast-moving number of paperbacks.

## Terry Hillyer

**Address**   301 Sydenham Road
              London
              SE26 5EW
**Tel**        020 8778 6361
**Fax**       020 8777 2506
**Opening hours**
Tues, Thurs, Fri 9.30am – 4pm, Sat 9.30am – 2pm

In among the mixture of antiques and bric-a-brac you will find a reasonable selection of secondhand and antiquarian books.

## Tlon Books

**Branch**   The Apprentice Shop
              Merton Abbey Mills
              London
              SW19 2RD
**Tel**        020 8540 4371
**Opening hours**
Mon-Sun 11am – 6pm

**Branch**   Elephant and Castle
              Shopping Centre
              London
              SE1
**Tel**        020 7701 0360
**Opening hours**
Mon-Sun 9am – 6pm

Both shops offer an excellent range of secondhand books with most popular subject areas covered. The Merton shop is particularly strong in academic subjects.

## Unsworths Booksellers

**Address**    12 Bloomsbury Square
London
WC1B 3QA
**Tel**    020 7436 9836
**Fax**    020 7637 7334
**Web**
www.unsworths.com
**Email**
books@unsworths.com
**Opening hours**
Mon-Sat 10am – 8pm, Sun noon – 8pm
**Services**
Catalogues

In the last edition we praised the good-value books on academic subjects and the arts and a visit to Unsworths will confirm that nothing has changed in that field. It remains a bright and modern shop with a newly expanded antiquarian section downstairs and continues to be the best places to come for low-price scholarly and academic books.

## Vortex Books

**Address**    139-141 Church Street
Stoke Newington
London
N16 0UH
**Tel**    020 7254 6516
**Opening hours**
Mon-Fri 11am – 6pm, Sat 10am – 6pm, Sun noon – 6pm

Part of a complex including a café and jazz bar, the bookshop deals in the humanities and more general topics with a few first editions.

## Walden Books

**Address**    38 Harmond Street
London
NW1 8DP
**Tel**    020 7267 8146
**Opening hours**
Thurs-Sun 10.30am – 6.30pm

Located off Chalk Farm Road and opposite the bus garage. Carries a general stock with an emphasis on the arts and literature with paperbacks prominent.

## Woburn Bookshop

**Address**    10 Woburn Walk
London
WC1H 0JL
**Tel**    020 7388 7278

*See Politics & Social Sciences*

## World's End Bookshop

**Address**    357 Kings Road
London
SW3 5ES
**Tel**    020 7352 9376
**Opening hours**
Mon-Sun 10am – 6.30pm
**Services**
Catalogues

At the far end of the King's Road close to the World's End pub is the home to a good selection of secondhand books mainly concentrating on arts and literature. They also have a small selection of antiquarian books and first editions.

# *Sport*

**Boxing • Cricket • Football • Golf • Horses & Horse Racing • Polo**

## Blacklock's Bookshop

**Address**  8 Victoria Street
Englefield Green
Egham
Surrey
TW20 0QY
**Tel**  01784 438025
**Opening hours**
Mon-Sat 9am – 5pm
**Services**
Catalogues

Located in exactly the right area for their specialisation this small, mainly secondhand, bookshop has Britain's largest stock of books on polo. They produce two polo catalogues a year, winter and summer, and are clearly experts in their field.

## Extra Cover

**Address**  101 Boundary Road
St Johns Wood
London
NW8 0RG
**Tel**  020 7625 1191
**Opening hours**
Tues-Sat 10am – 5.30pm, Sun 10am – 2pm

A specialist in secondhand books on cricket and football with prints, programmes, scorecards and other sporting ephemera available too. It's always a good place to try for old copies of *Wisden Almanack* or *Rothmans Football Yearbook*, as it is for club histories, however there is a tendency for many books to be priced a lot higher than you might reasonably expect.

## Golfiana

**Address**   Grays-in-the-Mews
Davies Mews
London
W1
**Tel**   020 7408 1239
**Fax**   020 7493 9344
**Opening hours**
Mon-Fri 10.30am – 5.30pm

A small unit in Grays Mews near to Bond Street underground. They cover all aspects of golfiana from ephemera, postcards, pictures, silver, ceramics, tin and diecast toys as well as a small selection of secondhand books.

## Horseman's Bookshop JA Allen

**Address**   4 Lower Grosvenor Place
Buckingham Palace Road
London
SW1W 0EL
**Tel**   020 7834 5606
**Fax**   020 7233 8001
**Web**
www.allens-books.com
**Email**
sales@allens-books.com
**Opening hours**
Mon-Fri 9am – 5pm, Sat 10am – 2pm
**Services**
Mail order, catalogues

J.A. Allen was founded in 1926 and has been at the present address opposite the Royal Mews since 1946. They deal exclusively in new, secondhand and rare books on everything to do with horses and equine pursuits. The range of stock and expertise is unrivalled and they produce regular catalogues.

## Lillywhites

**Address**   Book Department
Lillywhites
Piccadilly
London
SW1Y 4QF
**Tel**   020 7915 4000
**Opening hours**
Mon-Fri 10am – 8pm, Sat 9am – 7pm, Sun 11am – 5pm

Within this internationally known sports store selling a huge range of sports clothing and equipment there is a sports bookshop. It stocks a reasonable range of sports books, with a particular strength in fitness and technique, but Sportspages has slightly more to offer the general sports fan.

## The London Yacht Centre

**Address**   13 Artillery Lane
London
E1 7LP
**Tel**   020 7247 2047
**Opening hours**
Mon-Fri 9am – 5.30pm, Sat 10am – 3pm

Founded in 1957 as a general yacht chandlers and now one of the leaders in the country. The shop is only two minutes' walk from Liverpool Street station and carries an extensive range of yachting hardware, electronic equipment and clothing. There is a selective range of associated publications on technical aspects of yachting and cruising, including charts and guides.

# The Lord's Shop

**Address**  Lord's Ground
St John's Wood Road
London
NW8 8QN
**Tel**  020 7432 1021
**Fax**  020 7432 1007
**Web**
(The Lord's site) www.lords.org
**Opening hours**
Mon-Fri 10am – 5pm, Sat, Sun 10am –
4.30 match days (from noon if not)

Stocks a wide range of cricket
equipment, merchandise, memorabilia and a comprehensive selection
of cricket books. Combine a visit to
the shop with a tour of the most
famous cricket ground in the world
(020 7432 1033 for details) and
take in the excellent museum too.

# JW McKenzie

**Address**  12 Stoneleigh Park Road
Ewell
Epsom
Surrey
KT19 0QT
**Tel**  020 8393 7700
**Fax**  020 7939 1694
**Opening hours**
Mon-Fri 9.30am – 5pm
**Services**
Mail order

You need to be a cricket connois-
seur and an avid collector to seek
out and appreciate J.W. McKenzie,
probably the world's leading
specialist in secondhand, antiquarian and rare cricket books. They
serve customers all over the world
united by the love of cricket and
writing on the game. Whether you

are looking for a county history, an
obscure collection of cricket writing
or the rarest of antiquarian volumes
from the earliest days of the game,
your best chance of finding it is to
call here.

# The Oval Shop

**Address**  The Foster's Oval
Kennington
London
SE11 5SS
**Tel**  020 7820 1866
**Fax**  020 7735 7769
**Opening hours**
Mon-Fri 10am – 4pm

Conveniently situated at the main
entrance to the ground and packed
with cricket clothing, equipment,
books and a small number of
cricket videos.

# Rowland Wards

**Address**  Holland and Holland
31-33 Bruton Street
London
W1X 8JB
**Tel**  020 7499 4411
**Fax**  020 7499 4544
**Opening hours**
Mon-Fri 9.30am – 5.30pm

*See Countries*

# Sporting Bookshop

**Address**  97 Wood Street
Walthamstow
London
E17 3HX
**Tel**  020 8521 9803
**Opening hours**
Mon-Wed, Fri 9.30am – 4.15pm,
Thurs, Sat 9.30am – 5pm

Always guaranteed to contain an interesting choice of secondhand and antiquarian books on a wide range of sports. Football books and programmes, cricket and boxing are the main specialisations.

## Sportspages

**Address**    Caxton Walk
              94-96 Charing Cross Road
              London
              WC2H 0JG
**Tel**        020 7240 9604
**Fax**        020 7836 0104
**Web**
www.sportspages.co.uk
**Opening hours**
Mon-Sat 9.30am – 7pm

A huge range of books on the wonderful world of sport accompanied by a comprehensive selection of magazines and videos. Naturally, football predominates – especially the unrivalled choice of fanzines – but everything else is covered too, including a baseball section that would put some bookshops the other side of the Atlantic to shame. Signing sessions are a regular feature with the result that the shop always has a number of signed books in stock for devotees to buy. They also have a branch in Manchester.

# Transport & Military

**Aviation • Buses • Manuals • Maritime • Military • Modelling
Motoring • Naval • Railways • Shipping • Trams**

## Anthony Cooke

**Address**   Unit 202
              Station House
              49 Greenwich High Road
              London
              SE10 8JLI
**Tel**       020 8694 1178
**Fax**       020 8694 1178
**Opening hours**
By appointment only

Mainly a mail order business specialising in all aspects of shipping. They do welcome visitors but it is advisable to telephone first.

## Anthony J Simmonds

**Address**   23 Nelson Road
              Greenwich
              London
              SE10 9JB
**Tel**       020 8853 1727
**Fax**       020 8305 0649
**Opening hours**
Mon-Sun 10am – 6pm
**Services**
Mail order, catalogues

Other bookshops in Greenwich tend to have a section of maritime books but this shop specialises exclusively in new, secondhand and antiquarian books on the subject of naval and maritime history, yachting and voyages. It is appropriately located between the naval museum and the local church in a fine listed building. The stock is varied, priced from 50p to £5,000, and you can be assured of friendly service. Two specialist catalogues are produced every year and sent to customers world wide, many of whom discovered the shop on a visit to the museum.

## Aviation Bookshop

**Address**    656 Holloway Road
              London
              N19 3PD
**Tel**        020 7272 3630
**Fax**        020 7272 9761
**Opening hours**
Mon-Sat 9.30am – 5.30pm
**Services**
Mail order, catalogues

A shop dedicated to aviation and all its aspects and claims to be the only such shop in Europe. It was founded in 1948 and has since become established as an authority on all aeronautical topics. They stock both new and secondhand books along with a vast range of magazines, technical plans, videos, posters and photographs. The interior is appropriately decorated with model aircraft and attracts visiting enthusiasts from all over the world. A complete catalogue of all new books is available but the secondhand stock is too large to list.

## Booking Hall

**Address**    7 Charlotte Place
              London
              W1P 1AQ
**Tel**        020 7255 2123
**Opening hours**
Mon-Fri 11am – 7pm, Sat 11am – 5pm
**Services**
Mail order, book search

Barely a minute from Goodge Street underground, the Booking Hall is well known to dedicated railway fans who can find over 2,000 titles on their passion. Railways of the British Isles is the main area of expertise along with the London underground, buses and trams. The selection of ephemera is fascinating with leaflets, timetables and old magazines. A station board or old name plate may occasionally be seen alongside the regular stock of models.

## Books Bought and Sold

**Address**    68 Walton Road
              East Molesey
              Surrey
              KT8 0DL
**Tel**        020 8224 3232
**Fax**        020 8224 3576
**Opening hours**
Tues-Sat 10am – 5pm

This general secondhand bookshop is particularly strong on motoring, aviation, railways, military and illustrated children's books.

## Chaters

**Address**    8 South Street
              Isleworth
              Middlesex
              TW7 7DH
**Tel**        020 8568 9750
**Fax**        020 8569 8273
**Opening hours**
Mon-Sat 9am – 5.30pm
**Services**
Mail order, catalogues, book search

This premises has been a bookshop for over 60 years and started life selling fiction. In the late '50s it began to deal solely in all forms of transport and entered the next decade as a specialist dedicated to motoring and motorcycling. They aim to stock every book in print and most of those that are no longer available new. All UK-published books are carried with a large American selection and other European titles where the home grown is not sufficient. The range of videos is unrivalled and the out-of-print section accommodates over 200 feet of shelving packed with the best stock anywhere. Behind the scenes lurk back issues of motoring magazines dating from the turn of the century. Chaters repeatedly comes to the rescue by providing the missing link to restorers and owners and the motoring press frequently use the shop as a reference source. Circuit shops operate at the major tracks on race days and other major motoring events are attended by the mobile book-stall.

## Connoisseur Car Books

**Address**   11a Devonshire Road
London
W4
**Tel**   020 8742 0022
**Fax**   020 8742 0360
**Web**
www.chariot.co.uk
**Email**
chariot.@easynet.co.uk

**Opening hours**
Mon-Sat 10am – 6pm
**Services**
Mail order, catalogues

The joys of motoring is the theme of this particular bookshop which deals in all aspects of motoring with a stock of both new and second-hand books, many of which are rare or out of print.

## Falconwood Transport and Military Bookshop

**Address**   5 Falconwood Parade
The Green
Welling
Kent
DA16 2PL
**Tel**   020 8303 8291
**Fax**   020 8303 8291
**Web**
falconwood@golobalnet.co.uk
**Opening hours**
Thurs-Sat 9.30am – 5.30pm, other days appointment only
**Services**
Mail order, catalogues

Tricky to locate but once you get there it is heaven for all transport and military buffs. Secondhand books galore on aviation, motoring, railways and maritime transport. There is also a range of military titles.

## Francis Edwards

**Address**   13 Great Newport Street
off Charing Cross Road
London
WC2H 7JA
**Tel**   020 7379 7669
**Fax**   020 7836 5977

**Email**
sales@femilitary.demon.co.uk
**Opening hours**
Mon-Sat 9.30am – 6.30pm
**Services**
Mail order, catalogues

A small stock of antiquarian and secondhand books on military and maritime subjects amongst a fairly sparse general range of books.

## Ian Allen Transport Bookshop

**Address**   45-46 Lower Marsh
Waterloo
London
SE1 7RG
**Tel**   020 7401 2100
**Fax**   020 7401 2887
**Opening hours**
Mon-Sat 9am – 5.30pm
**Services**
Mail order

Ian Allen was a trainspotter whose passion led him to becoming a leading publisher and bookseller. Transport on the road, track, rail, in the air and on the water is covered here in its entirety. The inevitable overlap into matters military is also handled comprehensively. There are model trains, cars, magazines, catalogues and a notice board to disseminate information to the faithful.

## Imperial War Museum

**Address**   Lambeth Road
London
SE1 6HZ
**Tel**   020 7416 5000

**Opening hours**
Mon-Sun 10am – 6pm

An attractive shop located in one of London's most popular and interesting museums. Over 2,000 books are stocked on 20th-century military history and conflict. The emphasis is firmly on the two major wars but other contemporary conflicts are covered. What sets this shop apart from others in this field is the range of educational titles. As is the case with all museum shops there is a full range of gifts to buy here, not all with a military theme.

## ISO Publications

**Address**   137 Westminster Bridge
Road
London
SE1 7HR
**Tel**   020 7261 9588
**Fax**   020 7261 1877
**Opening hours**
Mon-Fri 9.30am – 5.30pm, Sat 10am – 3pm
**Services**
Mail order, catalogues

A small shop stuffed with a huge selection of books on every aspect of military, aviation and naval topics. There is also a good selection on modelling and model engineering to complete a comprehensive stock range. ISO is also a publisher of military books and their range is available here in its entirety.

## Lens of Sutton

**Address**   4 Westmead Road
Sutton
Surrey
SM1 4JT
**Tel**   020 8642 0981
**Opening hours**
Mon-Sat 11am – 6pm (Wed 11am – 2pm)
**Services**
Mail order

A corner shop, in business since 1929, that has a comprehensive range of books and periodicals on buses, trams and railways. Titles as diverse as *Steam in Australia* to *Railways through the Chilterns* hark back to the glory days of steam and trams. To complement the books they also stock a number of Dinky, Matchbox and Corgi models of cars, trucks and buses.

## London Transport Museum

**Address**   The Piazza
Covent Garden
London
WC2E 7BB
**Tel**   020 7379 6344
**Opening hours**
Mon-Sun 10am – 6pm

The museum houses a collection of historic buses, trams, trolley buses and underground trains with a fascinating range of ephemera and art. The shop reflects the museum contents and carries titles on road and rail transport in general with a special emphasis on London past and present. The shop is a treasure trove of gift ideas based on London transport's unique poster images.

## Marine Society

**Address**   202 Lambeth Road
London
SE1 7JW
**Tel**   020 7261 9535
**Fax**   020 7401 2537
**Web**
www.marinesociety.org.uk
**Email**
enq@marinesociety.org.uk
**Opening hours**
Mon-Fri 9.15am – 4.45pm
**Services**
Mail order

A place for serious seafarers, dealing only with technical texts, guides and manuals associated with merchant seamen's professional examinations. The business is primarily mail order so please ring first.

## Military History Bookshop

**Address**   77-81 Bell Street
London
NW1 6TA
**Tel**   020 7723 2095
**Fax**   020 7723 4665
**Web**
www.militaryhistorybooks.com
**Email**
sales@tmhbs.force9.co.uk
**Opening hours**
By appointment only
**Services**
Mail order, catalogues

A real find for the military enthusiast, this specialist bookshop is completely devoted to military matters. Most of the business is mail order but browsers are welcome and staff will happily show you round. The range is huge and highly specialised: books include new and secondhand covering such subjects as Finnish Army uniforms from 1936 to 1970 to head-dress badges of the British Army from the year dot to the present. Having been around for over 25 years they know their stuff and will attempt to find any book within this field.

## Motor Books

**Address** 33 and 36 St Martins Court
London
WC2N 4AL
**Tel** 020 7836 6728
**Fax** 020 7497 2539
**Opening hours**
Mon-Fri 9.30am – 6pm (Thurs 9.30am – 7pm), Sat 10.30am – 5.30pm
**Services**
Catalogues

Has been serving motoring enthusiasts from this St Martins Court location for 40 years or so. Aviation, military, railways and maritime subjects have been added over the years as shops next door to the original have been acquired. They claim to be world leaders in current books on motoring, railways, maritime, military and aviation and packed shelves are testament to the claim that there are 50,000 books in stock. Specialist catalogues cover a lot of ground but a personal visit is essential.

## National Army Museum Shop

**Address** Royal Hospital Road
Chelsea
London
SW3 4HT
**Tel** 020 7730 0717
**Fax** 020 7823 6573
**Opening hours**
Mon-Sun 10am – 5.30pm

Pleasantly located adjacent to the Royal Hospital in Chelsea. The shop carries a small range of books on all aspects of military history and soldiering through the ages and operates as a gift shop to visitors to this fascinating museum.

## Smokebox

**Address** 3 Cromwell Road
Kingston upon Thames
Surrey
KT2 6RF
**Tel** 020 8549 9700
**Opening hours**
Tues-Sat 10.30am – 6pm
**Services**
Mail order

A small shop crammed with secondhand books and magazines from floor to ceiling. Searching things out can be quite difficult but help from the resident expert is always on hand. While books on railways (hence the shop name) and buses make up the bulk of the stock, they do cover most other modes of transport.

## The London Yacht Centre

**Address**   13 Artillery Lane
London
E1 7LP
**Tel**   020 7247 2047
**Opening hours**
Mon-Fri 9am – 5.30pm, Sat 10am – 3pm

*See Sport*

## Warehouse Publications

**Address**   5 Rathbone Square
Tanfield Road
Croydon
CR0 1BT
**Tel**   020 8681 3031
**Web**
www.warehouse.co.uk
**Email**
pat@warehouse.co.uk
**Opening hours**
Mon-Fri 8am – 5pm (by appointment)

**Services**
Mail order, catalogues

A highly specialised outfit dealing solely in books on military and commercial vehicles. They are mainly mail order but do welcome visitors by appointment.

## World of Transport

**Address**   37 Heath Road
Twickenham
Middlesex
TW1
**Tel**   020 8891 3169
**Opening hours**
Mon-Fri 9.30am – 5.30pm, Sat 9.30am – 5pm
**Services**
Mail order, catalogues

The shop is close to the railway station and covers air, road and rail transport to the tune of 4,000 book titles in stock as well as videos on the same topics.

*Notes*

# *Travel*

## Atlases • Exploration • Guides • Maps •Ordnance Survey • Voyages

## Atlas Books

**Address**  55-57 Tabernacle Street
London
EC2A 4AA
**Tel**  020 7490 4540
**Fax**  020 7490 4514
**Web**
www.atlasgallery.com
**Email**
bn@atlasgallery.com
**Opening hours**
Mon-Fri 10am – 5.30pm
**Services**
Mail order, catalogues

In this gallery of old travel
photographs and prints you will
find first edition travel books and
general texts on photography.

## Beaumont Travel Books

**Address**  31 Museum Street
London
W1CA
**Tel/Fax**  020 7637 5862
**Web**
www.antiquarian.com/beaumont-
travel-books
**Email**
beaumont@antiquarian.com
**Opening hours**
Mon-Sat 10.30am – 6pm
**Services**
Catalogues

Antiquarian, rare and secondhand
books on travel the world over are
the subject of choice in this authoritative bookshop. You could easily
spend hours browsing here, not just

because there is so much to look at, because you have to ask to leave the shop so a member of staff can operate the door buzzer to let you back on the street.

## Bernard J Shapero Rare Books

**Address**   32 St George Street
London
W1R 0EA
**Tel**          020 7493 0876
**Fax**          020 7229 7860
**Web**
www.shapero.com
**Email**
rarebooks@shapero.com
**Opening hours**
Mon-Fri 9.30am – 6.30pm, Sat 11am – 5pm
**Services**
Mail order, events, catalogues, signings

A well-established antiquarian specialist occupying attractive premises. Voyages and travel and associated literature are the main specialisation. Natural history is also well covered within the fine selection of lovely books.

## Daunt Books

**Address**   193 Haverstock Hill
London
NW3
**Tel**          020 7794 4006
**Fax**          020 7431 2732
**Opening hours**
Mon-Sat 10am – 9pm, Sun 11am – 7pm

A sister shop to the main travel bookshop located on Marylebone Road. Has a similar stock profile but is naturally restricted due to its size.

## Daunt Books for Travellers

**Address**   83 Marylebone High Street
London
W1M 3DE
**Tel**          020 7224 2295
**Fax**          020 7224 6893
**Opening hours**

Mon-Sat 9am – 7pm

Natural light pours through the skylights running down the centre of this attractive shop. The books are arranged by country so that all those relating to one particular country are easily found in one place. Travel guides sit alongside books on the food, culture and fiction of the country, providing a complete and unique selection. This common-sense strategy benefits the customer and all travel sections should be ordered this way. Simply a great shop to spend hours in.

## Geographers

**Address**   44 Grays Inn Road
London
WC1X 8LR
**Tel**          020 7440 9500
**Opening hours**
Mon-Fri 9am – 5pm

The shop window for the publisher of the well known A–Z guides, maps and atlases. This is the place to find the complete range.

## National Map Centre

**Address**   22-24 Caxton Street
London
SW1H 0QU
**Tel**       020 7222 2466
**Fax**       020 7222 2619
**Opening hours**
Mon-Fri 9am – 6pm

This is Great Britain's premier Ordnance Survey agent. Whether a suburb, town or country in the UK, the most detailed maps available can be found here. In addition to motoring and touring maps, street plans, travel guides and wall maps there is a specialist service for professionals and business.

## Nomad Books

**Address**   781 Fulham Road
London
SW6 5HA
**Tel**       020 7736 4000
**Fax**       020 7736 9454
**Web**
www.nomadbooks.com
**Opening hours**
Mon-Fri 9am – 8pm, Sat 10am – 6pm,
Sun 11am – 5pm
**Services**
Mail order, events, readings

Just a short walk from Parsons Green underground will lead you to Nomad Books where a whole floor is devoted to travel books. As well as being a travel specialist this is also a fine example of a local general bookshop with a good range and friendly service. The selection of contemporary fiction paperbacks is good with other popular subjects prominent too.

## Reg & Philip Remington

**Address**   18 Cecil Court
Charing Cross Road
London
WC2N 4HE
**Tel**       020 7836 9771
**Fax**       020 7497 2526
**Opening hours**
Mon-Fri 9am – 5pm

Serious antiquarian and second-hand books on voyages and travel with some engravings.

## Robert Frew

**Address**   106 Great Russell Street
London
WC1B 3NA
**Tel**       020 7580 2311
**Fax**       020 7580 2313

*See Antiquarian*

## Stanford's

**Branch**    12-14 Long Acre
Covent Garden
London
WC2C 9LP
**Tel**       020 7836 1321
**Fax**       020 7836 0169
**Opening hours**
Mon-Fri 9am – 7.30pm, Sat 10am – 7pm
**Services**
Mail order, events, signings, catalogues

**Branch**    Stanford's at Campus Travel
52 Grosvenor Gardens
Victoria
London
SW1W 0AG
**Tel**       020 7730 1314
**Fax**       020 7730 1354
**Opening hours**
Mon-Fri 9am – 6pm, Sat 10am – 5pm

**Branch** Stanford's
British Airways
156 Regent Street
London
W1R 5TA
**Tel** 020 7434 4744
**Fax** 020 7434 4636
**Opening hours**
Mon-Fri 9.30am – 6pm, Sat 10am – 4pm

The name of Stanford's has been synonymous with maps and travel since Edward Stanford, cartographer and printer, started the business in 1852. It is the world's premier source of maps and guides and whether you're crossing the Sahara or trekking the Himalayas it is likely that the map or guide to help you out came from Stanford's. They also have a satellite branch, backed up by all the expertise and stock range of the Covent Garden store, in the Campus Travel agency and another at British Airways on Regent Street.

## Trailfinders

**Address** 194 Kensington High Street
London
W8 7RG
**Tel** 020 7938 3999
**Opening hours**
Mon-Sat 9am – 6pm

This well-known travel agency and flight booker has a nicely stocked travel book department so they can give you expert advice, book your ticket, stab your arm in the clinic and sell you the right book to ensure you're fully prepared for the trip ahead. The result is a one-stop shop for travellers.

## Travel Bookshop

**Address** 13 Blenheim Crescent
London
W11 2EE
**Tel** 020 7229 5260
**Fax** 020 7243 1552
**Web**
www.thetravelbookshop.co.uk
**Email**
sales@thetravelbookshop.demon.co.uk
**Opening hours**
Mon-Sat 10am – 6pm
**Services**
Mail order, events, readings

Often described as 'the perfect travel bookshop' and a visit will quickly prove the accuracy of such a claim to fame. The stock covers maps, guides, histories and travel writing both new and secondhand and the shop is located in the lovely Blenheim Crescent alongside the Garden Bookshop and opposite Books for Cooks.

## YHA Shop

**Address** 14 Southampton Street
Covent Garden
WC2E 7HY
**Tel** 020 7836 8541
**Fax** 020 7836 8263
**Opening hours**
Mon-Fri 10am – 7pm, Sat 9am – 6.30pm, Sun 11am – 5pm

There is a travel bookshop inside the Youth Hostel Association shop which sells primarily outdoor clothing and equipment. Concentrating on maps and guides – with YHA publications too – the stock is wide ranging enough to make this an excellent source of travel info.

# Area Index

## Central London

# Inner London

# Outer London

## North

| | | | |
|---|---|---|---|
| Barnet | WH Smith | Chains | 59 |
| Enfield | Felicity J Warnes | Crafts & Pastimes | 92 |
| | Ottakar's | Chains | 53 |
| | Toys and Tales | Children's | 69 |
| | Wesley Owen | Religion & Theology | 168 |
| | WH Smith | Chains | 60 |
| Potters Bar | Elaine's | General | 110 |

## North West

| | | | |
|---|---|---|---|
| Borehamwood | Book Exchange | Secondhand | 173 |
| Chorleywood | Chorleywood Bookshop | General | 107 |
| Eastcote | Eastcote Bookshop | General | 109 |
| | Hammond Roberts | General | 112 |
| Edgware | Carmel Gifts | Religion & Theology | 156 |
| | WH Smith | Chains | 59 |
| Harrow | Harrow School Bookshop | Academic | 12 |
| | Marylebone Books | Academic | 14 |
| | WH Smith | Chains | 60 |
| Ickenham | Hayes Bookshop | Secondhand | 178 |
| Northwood | Christian Book Centre | Religion & Theology | 158 |
| Pinner | Children's Bookshop | Children's | 65 |
| | Comparative Religion Centre | Religion & Theology | 159 |
| | Corbett's Bookshop | General | 108 |
| Ruislip | Bookshop, The | General | 105 |
| | WH Smith | Chains | 61 |
| Uxbridge | Bargain Books | Secondhand | 172 |
| | Barnards Bookshop Ltd | General | 102 |
| | James Thin | Chains | 52 |
| | Marantha Christian Bookshop | Religion & Theology | 163 |
| | Waterstone's | Academic | 16 |
| | WH Smith | Chains | 61 |
| Wealdstone | Wesley Owen | Religion & Theology | 168 |

## North East

| | | | |
|---|---|---|---|
| Ilford | Bible Bookshop | Religion & Theology | 156 |
| | Centre for Peace | Religion & Theology | 157 |
| | Edward Terry Bookseller | Secondhand | 175 |
| | Masters Christian Books | Religion & Theology | 163 |
| | Volume One | Chains | 52 |
| | Waterstone's | Chains | 55 |
| Loughton | Bookshop | General | 105 |

| Epsom | Dovecote Christian Bookshop | Religion & Theology | 160 |
| | Waterstone's | Chains | 55 |
| Ewell | J W McKenzie | Sport | 187 |
| New Malden | Cannings | General | 107 |
| | WH Smith | Chains | 60 |
| Sutton | Altered Images | Comics & Science Fiction | 71 |
| | Baines Bookshop | General | 102 |
| | Kendrake Children's Bookshop | Children's | 67 |
| | Lens of Sutton | Transport & Military | 193 |
| | Paperback Exchange | Secondhand | 180 |
| | Waterstone's | Chains | 56 |
| | Wesley Owen | Religion & Theology | 168 |
| | WH Smith | Chains | 61 |

## South West

| Chertsey | Glasheens Bookshop | Secondhand | 177 |
| East Molesey | Books Bought and Sold | Transport & Military | 190 |
| | Embroiderers' Guild Bookshop | Crafts & Pastimes | 91 |
| Egham | Blacklock's Bookshop | Sport | 185 |
| | Waterstone's, *Royal Holloway* | Academic | 17 |
| Hampton | Ian Sheridan Bookshop | Secondhand | 178 |
| Kew | The Kew Shop | Crafts & Pastimes | 93 |
| | Lloyd's of Kew | Crafts & Pastimes | 93 |
| Kingston | Alkitab Bookshop | Countries | 79 |
| | Bookworld | General | 106 |
| | Chapter and Verse | Religion & Theology | 157 |
| | Dillons, *Bentall Centre* | Chains | 51 |
| | Fun Learning, *Bentall Centre* | Children's | 66 |
| | John Lewis | Children's | 67 |
| | Smokebox | Transport & Military | 194 |
| | Waterstone's, *Kingston University* | Academic | 18 |
| | Waterstone's, *Thames Street* | Chains | 56 |
| | WH Smith, *Bentall Centre* | Chains | 60 |
| Richmond | Houbens Bookshop | General | 113 |
| | Kew Bookshop | General | 114 |
| | Lion and Unicorn Bookshop | Children's | 67 |
| | Richmond Bookshop | Secondhand | 181 |
| | Waterstone's | Chains | 56 |
| | Wesley Owen | Religion & Theology | 168 |
| | WH Smith, *George Street* | Chains | 61 |
| | WH Smith, *Station* | Chains | 61 |
| Staines | Canaan Christian Book Centre | Religion & Theology | 156 |
| | Ottakar's | Chains | 53 |
| | WH Smith | Chains | 61 |
| Surbiton | Christian Bookshop | Religion & Theology | 158 |
| Twickenham | Anthony C Hall | Countries | 80 |
| | Langton's Bookshop | General | 115 |

## West

# Bookshop Index

# Bookshop Index

# Bookshop Index

# Bookshop Index